EASTWARD
the CONVOYS

By the Same Author:

ASHES IN THE WILDERNESS
THE CAT IN THE CONVOY
PAYOFF IN BLACK
THE DEER CRY
SEEK FOR A HERO
SIDEWALK STATESMAN
DESTROYERS—60 YEARS
TREASON TRAIL

William G. Schofield

EASTWARD
the CONVOYS

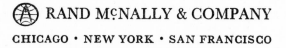

RAND McNALLY & COMPANY

CHICAGO • NEW YORK • SAN FRANCISCO

For Those
Who
Stood Watch

FOREWORD

IN THE FALL OF 1941, GERMAN SUBMARINES RULED the Atlantic Ocean and the waters beyond to the East.

They roamed at will along our coast from Maine to Texas. They torpedoed our unarmed merchant ships within sight of land. They mined our seaboard harbors. They put saboteurs ashore on beaches that already knew the red glare of flames at night and the wreckage of sunken ships and the sick-sweet smell of corpses.

In September of that year, the U-boats attacked the U.S.S. *Greer* off Iceland and sank the S.S. *Steel Seafarer* in the Red Sea. In October, near Iceland, they torpedoed the U.S.S. *Kearny* and the U.S.S. *Salinas,* and sank the U.S.S. *Reuben James.* The men and weapons that we were sending out in convoy were vanishing forever in the Atlantic graveyard.

This was part of Germany's strangulation strategy, designed to drive our merchant ships from the seas, thereby cutting off the shipments of war supplies to Europe and forcing the surrender of Great Britain.

But at this point, in October, 1941, the U. S. Navy organized its Armed Guard branch at Little Creek, Virginia to train Navy gun crews for duty aboard the nation's 1,375 merchant ships. Three weeks later in Novem-

ber, when Congress repealed the Neutrality Act of 1939,
Little Creek had 24 officers and 192 men ready to
board ship.

By the time World War II ended, the Armed Guard
program had expanded to West Coast and Gulf Coast
bases, and to the ports of all Allied nations. Navy gun
crews aboard merchant ships had fought through with
their cargoes upon all the combatant seas of the world
and had won literally thousands of decorations and com-
mendations for bravery. At a heavy cost of life, they had
delivered to foreign shores the millions of tons of supplies
and munitions without which the war against the Axis
Powers could not have been won.

This book, while not an Armed Guard history, is one
man's story of what it was like to be at sea in the memorable time of the convoys.

W.G.S.

CONTENTS

EASTWARD
the CONVOYS

CHAPTER ONE

THE LOST AND LONELY

WE SIGHTED THE TWO MEN ON THE RAFT JUST AT sundown that cold November evening, and we stared off at them and felt heartsick about it because we knew we were going to have to sail right on past and leave them to the sea, to the black, war-hungry North Atlantic.

Somebody had made the rule that when your ship was in convoy and running from submarines, you must not stop or turn aside for castaways. And in the early 1940's, when we were losing the Battle of the Atlantic to Admiral Doenitz and his U-boats, we had to obey such rules. It was the best way to keep the convoys afloat, and to carry out our mission of delivering the weapons of war to where they were needed. It was the best way to stay alive.

We had been fighting submarines that afternoon and as twilight fell we were scanning the sea with the glasses before darkness could come down and hide the enemy. That's when we caught sight of them. They were far, far off on the horizon, just two men feebly waving their shirts and occasionally jumping up and down on their raft.

I suppose they were shouting at us, crying out for help, cursing us in their frustration, but they were too

13

many miles away to be heard. So now we just stared at them through our binoculars, Simon and I, leaning on the starboard rail and looking far away to the eastward while the convoy held its formation and sailed steadily north.

"They look so lost," said Simon the signalman. "They look so lonely."

I said nothing. His words made me remember what we had been told at Little Creek, Virginia, where the Navy trained its Armed Guard gunners in early 1942, at the time when German submarines controlled the Atlantic, and the oil-stained wreckage of torpedoed ships fouled the eastern seaboard.

"When you leave here after three weeks of training," they had told us, "you will be Armed Guard Commanding Officers in charge of United States Navy gun crews aboard ships of the merchant marine. Many of you will be lost. All of you will be lonely."

Now it was many months and many voyages later, and perhaps those men on the faraway raft were two or more of our Little Creek alumni whose luck had finally run out. Or perhaps they were merchant seamen from a torpedoed convoy. Or survivors from a crippled submarine. There was no way of knowing anything about them except that they were two more victims of the Battle of the Atlantic who had to be ignored and abandoned by the passing convoy.

That was another thing the Navy had taught us at Little Creek, that and the lesson in how long to keep fighting.

"You will engage the enemy until your guns can no longer be fired," they had said. "That means until the decks are awash and the guns are going under. Then you may abandon ship if you wish. But you must never expect another convoy ship to stop and pick you up, nor may you permit your ship to stop for others. For the safety of the many, a ship in convoy must pass by all survivors in the sea. No stopping for anyone. Leave all rescues to the special rescue ships—if there are any."

So there it was, a reminder from the memory of the Little Creek lectures. Now there were two men on a raft out there, more than a thousand miles from land, fading from sight on a darkening horizon, and nobody would do anything to help them.

We watched them through the binoculars for as long as we could, until finally they merged with the approaching shadows and disappeared from sight. Shortly, it was blackout time and our ship, the S.S. *Gulfwing,* seemed to welcome the darkness as an enfolding blanket sent especially for wrapping around her hull and for hiding her cargo of petroleum from the fire of a submarine prowler.

It was lonely on the bridge that night, thinking of the two men on the raft. But at least we on *Gulfwing* were not lost, as they were—and as so many thousands of others would be before the war in the Atlantic came to an end.

For some reason, the memory of those two men on the raft has stayed alive through all the long years that have passed since the fighting stopped. So have other Armed Guard memories, of course, as probably they have with all the good men from Little Creek who, to borrow from the Bible, had business upon great waters and went down to the sea in ships.

Ours was a privileged company in a way, for it was our lot to be a Navy within a Navy, to roam the far seas and to know strange ports where the big fleets never ventured, to occupy a small world of our own in which we fought our personal, private war with submarines and aircraft. In that small world, and for what time was ours within it, we lived and fought and in turn either cursed or enjoyed war in a way that could never be understood by a sailor who had not experienced it.

We were denied the relaxing air of a warship's wardroom, where white-jacketed stewards usually keep the coffee percolating and where tradition supposedly forbade any talk about religion, politics, or women. Instead, we ate in the ship's saloon, whether we were on a tanker or a freighter, and it was a dull meal that didn't produce some kind of an exhilarating argument with merchant marine officers about any or all of the Navy's forbidden topics. We had free speech beyond anything the Bill of Rights ever embraced.

We were spared the Navy ban against taking a drink aboard ship. On the contrary, we usually joined the skipper and the first mate or chief engineer for two or three jiggers of Scotch before lunch, before dinner, and after every U-boat attack. It was good Scotch, too, government stock that we took aboard in Scotland at only $24 a case.

We had no Halsey or Nimitz or Spruance or Burke to lead us into battle and to send us congratulatory messages after the victory. Instead, we slogged along behind some anonymous officer known as the Escort Commander, in charge of our warship screen, and another known only as the Convoy Commodore, who was usually a retired Royal Navy admiral, reactivated through desperation and manpower shortage, and who sometimes didn't even know what we were shooting at from our column position miles away on the convoy's wing.

But that was all right. As long as they didn't bother us, we didn't bother them.

In short, our privilege was the privilege of informality and considerable freedom of action, of the right to fight our own war in our own way, of being so at-one with the great sea that it frequently cascaded down our necks, of being so close to the enemy in personal combat that sometimes we could smell his galley fumes and he ours (sauerkraut versus hickory-smoked bacon), and of celebrating safe arrival ashore by going with the skipper or the mate on a rollicking tour of the honky-tonk joints of Liverpool, Bristol, London, Alexandria, Suez, Algiers, or wherever that particular voyage happened to end.

In our early days at Little Creek, they never told us of all this. Perhaps they, the instructors, never knew about it. Perhaps they only knew that while many Armed Guard crews went to sea, many of them never returned. And they knew nothing, perhaps, of the wondrous and fascinating side of the convoy service—of exotic ports and strange sights, of a disappearing castle on the Irish headland, of ski trails in the Icelandic mountains, of slender sea snakes off the coast of Yemen, of the beautiful colors that glow when the rising sun touches the ocean caves of the Outer Hebrides, of soft and haunting music that floats out across the water at twilight from behind a Sahara dune, of mysterious balls of light that hover in the sky above the Arctic Circle.

All of this and much, much more was ours—all of this and the excitement of sweaty battle almost as raw and naked of modern defense as a throwback to the days of cutlass and chain shot. It was a man's life, and a good one. At times, in moments of sharp and poignant beauty, it was a poet's life as well.

But, of course, we never learned of this at Little Creek. There we learned only that our chances of getting home alive were somewhat less than those of a jungle message-runner who tries to take a shortcut through a river of crocodiles. The only ones in the Navy who suffered longer odds on the betting boards at Norfolk were the men of the Amphibious Forces who were training on another muddy patch of the Little Creek base. When we needed cheering up, we could always stroll over to where they were living in their tent villages and watch them brooding away their hours. Those visits always made us feel better.

Little Creek today is something of a country club among the Navy's bases. The Armed Guard crews have long since departed, not only from the base but from the Navy itself as well. The Amphibs of this day have taken it over and made it a place of comfort and beauty, with an excellent Officers Club.

We, too, had an Officers Club back in our day. It was very small and cramped, but if you complained about its size you were reminded that the death rate among Armed Guard officers was climbing every day. So why waste money enlarging a club for men who were being wiped out?

As though to support this argument, Little Creek saw to it that casualty lists were posted daily on the Officers Club bulletin board. Ships lost to submarines, ships lost to planes, officers known dead, officers missing and presumed to be dead, they were all posted there by name and date. Strangely enough, instead of stimulating moody drinking at the bar, this had a tendency to cause many officers to turn away cold sober and go out for a long walk in the night. In time, the casualty lists were discontinued, and those officers who were destined to die en route to Murmansk or Malta or London at least were sent on their way from Little Creek in a hangover haze of indifference.

The two most widely known slogans of the Armed Guard service adorned the Little Creek bar in those early days of training. They were the familiar: "Sighted sub. Glub, glub!" and the equally popular, "Ready, Aim, Abandon Ship!"

This was the atmosphere into which came the newly commissioned ensigns and lieutenants (jg) who were to train for command, assemble their gun crews of twenty to thirty inexperienced seamen and go forth upon the waters to keep as many merchant ships as possible from being sunk, and to deliver the weapons and supplies needed to carry on the war.

Since there were no doctors on the convoy ships, they also had to train to give emergency medical aid, from sewing up wounds to probing for chunks of shrapnel, and from setting a broken arm to treating a merchant radio officer for delirium tremens.

Once aboard ship, the Armed Guard Commanding Officer also was expected to be chaplain, school teacher for industrious seamen, diplomatic representative in foreign ports, mediator in disputes between merchant seamen and Navy gunners, censor of all personal mail, ship communications officer adept at flag hoists or blinker signal, intelligence officer and private eye in cases of attempted sabotage, custodian of classified security documents ("these must be destroyed before you die"), bartender and host for merchant officers visiting his quarters, referee for disputes arising from poker or blackjack or in-port love affairs, custodian of all Navy equipment from morphine syrettes to 5-inch shells, drinking partner and traveling companion for the ship's skipper ashore, postmaster for incoming and outgoing mail and—upon sounding General Quarters—commanding officer of the fighting ship until after the action ceased.

It was to fit him for these responsibilities—and for the overall responsibility for sixty lives and ten million dollars in war cargo each voyage—that Little Creek put him through its three-week training course.

Oddly enough, the short training exposure took hold. Probably one reason for this was that the average Armed Guard officer was older and more experienced than most other men of his rank. He was straight from civilian life— a lawyer, a sales director, a newspaper editor, a bank manager, a garage owner, a college professor, an architect, a football coach, an engineer. In short, he had lived more and learned to understand the peculiarities of human nature better than the Navy's younger officers who were just emerging from colleges and indoctrination schools. In the early days of the service, he was usually a family man, old enough to have stayed out of the war if he'd preferred. But he was in uniform by his own choice and he was in the Armed Guard, on convoy duty, only because he had volunteered for it. If he seldom complained at what came his way, it was because he knew he could blame nobody but himself. If he regretted his choice, he swallowed his regrets in silence. As a rule he was quietly content with his lot.

But many times he hated the things he had to do, such as watching two men on a raft as the dark of night came down and his ship plowed along on its course, abandoning them to the deep waters.

CHAPTER TWO

RAIDS AND REWARDS

THERE WERE MANY MEN WHO WENT OUT FROM Little Creek and died with their ships; sometimes they were men like Kenneth Muir or John Borum or Kenneth Willett.

A newcomer to the convoy service might hear their names and ask, who were they? what had they done? He would be told that in dying with their ships they had taught the rest of us how to live with ours—that we owed them much. We owed them our lives.

Somebody at a desk in Washington once wrote a long and wordy passage for the General Instructions booklet that was issued to all Armed Guard officers. He reminded them to be particularly careful to watch their language and their dress and the rights of their crew.

Perhaps this was a thoughtful thing for the Navy to do, but it was not at all necessary. Most officers learned on their first convoy crossing that the best language to use aboard a merchant ship in wartime usually was whatever brand of expression got the job done in the fastest possible time, regardless of etiquette or sensitive feelings. They also learned that the best way to dress was not necessarily the way the book said but was dictated by the best way to stay alive and comfortable, depending upon arctic blizzards, tropical hurricanes, fog, wind, and the momentary possibility of being exploded into the sea and spending the next week or two on a crowded life raft.

During the quiet hours in convoy, it took a long time to struggle through the official booklet and to digest all of its weighty advice. It took time that was doled out grudgingly, for it might have been spent to better advantage checking guns and life jackets, or drilling merchant seamen in their auxiliary jobs as ammunition passers. But the anonymous Washington author apparently felt confident that not many of his readers would be coming home to complain. He indicated as much when he concluded his remarks on a sailor's rights by pointing out:

"The officer whose constant interest in his men has been proved finds his men willing and ready to stand with him until the deck sinks below them."

That happened many times, of course. It also happened many times that the last ever seen of an Armed Guard officer was the sight of him driving his shipmates from a blazing, sinking wreck just before it went under and sucked him down to his death.

That was the way death came to Lt. (jg) Kenneth Muir, when his ship was sailing alone and was destroyed by a submarine in the Caribbean Sea.

It happened on a November night in 1942 when Muir's vessel—it was the S.S. *Nathaniel Hawthorne*—was nearing home port after a long and perilous voyage from the Persian Gulf. She had reached the waters just north of Trinidad when the lurking U-boat struck, slamming two torpedoes into her port side.

The *Nathaniel Hawthorne* exploded in a terrible blast of flame and hot steel, and she sank in less than two

minutes. Thirty-nine men died in that swift, roaring destruction. Ten survivors were picked up the next day by
a passing ship that was bound for New York. It was
through an interview on arrival in that port that one of the
survivors, an engine-room wiper, told in awed tones about
the cool bravery that Muir had shown in what must
have been a moment of terrible agony.

"I don't know how he could have been so calm," the
wiper said, shaking his head. "We were in the water and
we could see him in the light of the fire and the flares
that lit up the whole stern of the ship.

"We could see that one of his arms had been almost
blown clean off at the shoulder. I can't remember which
one, it was all so quick.

"But with his one good arm, he pushed three men to
the stern and made them jump clear of the ship. Then he
went back into the flames for more. We could see him
shouting, but we couldn't hear what he said; we saw he
was trying to get others to leap into the water.

"He must have been in terrible pain. But he stayed
with the ship. He didn't jump. In the end, he went down
with his gunners. I'm mighty proud to have served on a
ship with a guy that fine."

The Navy was proud of him too. They gave Muir the
Navy Cross posthumously, for extraordinary heroism.

Just as it was with Muir, for most of us from Little
Creek saving our ships and delivering our cargoes was
almost entirely a war fought against submarines or air
attack. But for a few others, it was different. Lt. (jg)
Kenneth M. Willett was one of those others. He fought
his last battle not against U-boats or planes but against
two enemy surface raiders that sent his ship to the

bottom. It was a courageous, heroic battle, although he must have known he never had a chance of being the winner.

When Willett's time came, he was in command of the Navy gun crew aboard the S.S. *Stephen Hopkins*. She was making her way unescorted from Capetown to Paramaribo on a lazy September day, when the two raiders disguised as friendly cargo ships came foaming over the South Atlantic horizon and bore down as though to join company. But the moment they closed within gun range, they slammed down their false hull plates and opened up on Willett's ship with a raking burst of shellfire.

One of the few survivors recalled that day's action:

"The two warships tore into us a little after noon. Mister Willett came out on deck just as the first shell exploded.

"He was hit almost immediately, and got seriously wounded by shrapnel from another shellburst. But he still managed to get back aft to the 4-inch gun. Back there at the stern, he directed the gun crew, and then he even stepped in and manned the gun himself. He kept pumping shells fast, especially into the raider that had the heaviest weapons.

"But both the warships kept firing back, and they battered us from stem to stern. Their shells hit our main boiler and cut our speed to one knot. They struck our radio mast and knocked down our antenna. They hit the steering-engine room and set it ablaze with incendiary shells. Then the main deckhouse caught it and broke into flames. We took a lot of hits below the waterline. The ship was all on fire and beginning to flood, and pretty soon she was going down by the stern.

"But all of this time, Mister Willett kept firing the 4-inch gun at close range. And he kept hitting his targets, too, mostly along the waterline, maybe thirty-five times. Both the raiders were badly damaged. We could see that one of them would probably go down.

"Then suddenly our magazine took a direct hit and exploded, and Mister Willett had to abandon his gun.

"Even then he wouldn't give up, though. He was badly wounded, but when he had to leave his gun he made his way down to the main deck. The last we saw of him there, he was trying to cut loose the life rafts to save the men who were in the sea. Then the ship plunged down out of sight, stern first, and he was gone."

Willett, like Muir, was given the Navy Cross posthumously. Later the Navy commissioned a new destroyer escort, U.S.S. *Kenneth M. Willett,* in his name.

And the Navy named other destroyer escorts for other men of that breed—for John Brennan, for William Herzog, for Hunter Marshall, for John R. Borum.

In Borum's case, to die with his doomed ship was particularly ironic, for he had already been responsible for saving the vessel once, when even her skipper had fled.

Borum was in command of the Navy crew aboard the tanker S.S. *Brilliant* when it was torpedoed in convoy on a November night east of Newfoundland.

The torpedo explosion ripped open the ship's starboard side and touched off a furious blaze in the spilling cargo of oil. The flames made a high, roaring fire in the predawn darkness. The ship's skipper, staring down from the bridge, took one look at the ugly inferno, tied down the "Abandon Ship" whistle, and led the race for the lifeboats.

Borum apparently saw no reason for the panic. He went groping around through the smoke, and somewhere amidships he ran into Third Mate J. C. Cameron, who by then was the only merchant officer left on deck.

"Look here," Borum said, "this is ridiculous. Why don't you just shut off that whistle and try putting out the fire?"

Cameron nodded agreeably, as though the idea somehow delighted him. "Why not?" he said. "Let's do it."

With the help of several men from the engine room, they did.

Four nights later, limping along at three knots, they reached harbor safely at St. John's. There the Newfoundland workers spent weeks doing a temporary patch-up job on the *Brilliant,* and then they sent for a tug to tow her to Halifax for full repairs.

But the *Brilliant* never made it. She set out from St. John's in the middle of January, 1943, and ran straight into an arctic gale that tossed her about until she snapped her towline. She was badly crippled, and in no shape at all to withstand the crashing waves and the brutal winds of the storm. She broke up that night and went to the bottom. And Borum went down with her.

Naturally, as an Armed Guard officer of the Little Creek alumni, you thought often of those men who had died. You thought of them especially in the long nights and stormy days upon the great waters of the North Atlantic, for that was where most of them gave up their lives. And you wondered when it might happen to you.

Sometimes they were men you had known, men who had trained with you on the rickety gun-loading machines in the Little Creek drill shed during the hot and dusty afternoons, or men who had joined you in the cool of the evening to roll dice for drinks at the bar. You remembered them the way they had been aboard the tired old gunboat U.S.S. *Dubuque,* sitting out in the middle of Chesapeake Bay and waiting for the morning fog to burn off so that they could run a green crew through its first target practice "at sea." You thought of them and wondered if the casualty lists were still being posted in the Officers Club.

You thought of them, too, as you sat in your cabin during quiet convoy hours and read the voyage reports of other Armed Guard officers, and wondered how many paths had crossed and crisscrossed on the sea lanes of the world, and how many would lead back home when the final voyage report had been written.

Sometimes, in those reports, they said so much by saying so little:

"We passed through heavy ice fields and while making an emergency turn in a blizzard to get out of the ice, stern lights were lit and regular fog signals were sounded. At 1235, the Convoy Commodore's ship was torpedoed and sank in less than one minute. We were next in column, and we passed a number of survivors in the water, about thirty of them. For the next few days the weather was overcast with snow flurries. Early in the morning, the convoy was attacked by four torpedo planes, but no ships were hit. At about 1300 hours, enemy surface craft were sighted. Our four accompanying destroyers immediately laid a smoke screen on the side from which they were approaching, and all merchant ships equipped with smoke pots lit them off. There were three German destroyers in the enemy group and they made five attempts to destroy our convoy but were driven off each time. During the battle, one of our ships was hit and sunk. Later the convoy passed through a thick ice pack and escaped in a heavy snowstorm. . . ."

That would have been the 1942 Murmansk run, probably, or beyond and up to Archangel.

Meanwhile, there was the Mediterranean to consider:

"Our ship was part of the invasion force and went in close to the beach with the original landing. We were subjected to shelling from enemy land positions which continued for seven days. The Germans increased their counter-action by frequent and heavy air attacks. Our ship was in the invasion area for eight days, and during this time we had twenty-seven actual bombings from enemy aircraft. The gun crew was on emergency watch for those eight days, obtaining very little rest and eating at irregular hours. In the heaviest air attack, bombers and fighter-bombers came over in full strength. Bombs were dropping throughout the bay as well as on the shore. The antiaircraft fire from this ship set up an effective barrage, but shrapnel flew about and several gunners were wounded. What looked like an enemy ME-109 came diving at our ship. The gunners filled her with 20-millimeter shells and the plane burst into flame, crashing into the ship's side and exploding as she hit. The explosion caused extensive internal damage, buckling the ship's engine-room plates, and destroying the generators. We were deprived of our electric power for several days and had no sanitary plumbing facilities left and no fresh water supply. During this time, the gunners stayed at their stations, awaiting a return attack. The ship took water rapidly and was listing to port, so we ran her onto the beach to avoid sinking. When the ship was beached, most of the merchant crew was taken off and put ashore. The Navy gun crew stayed at their battle stations, sleeping and eating there, so that the ship might be protected and the cargo that was so badly needed on the beach could be safely discharged. . . ."

Reading such reports and wondering about the friends you had known, it occurred to you sometimes that the instruction booklet we read at Little Creek, had not had much to say about what to do among icebergs and petroleum fires and broken plumbing facilities.

Those were things we had to learn for ourselves.

And perhaps we learned best from those who had died while learning.

CHAPTER THREE

GRAY LADY

WHEN YOU GIVE YOUR HEART TO A SHIP, YOU GIVE IT for all time. If you have chosen well, she seems to have a way of knowing it and of being eager to respond. When that happens, you are hers and she is yours, and the pairing is something that grows deep-felt and beautiful and a little sad.

Gulfwing and I were like that. Somehow we became a part of each other and necessary to each other, and when I finally had to leave her it was like walking out on a true love affair. I felt like a churl.

She had been around a lot before we met. You could tell that with one look at her; she showed the tattletale signs that come from living dangerously and from keeping on the go to the point of near-exhaustion.

But she carried herself well and with pride. The way she came in from the sea and moved gracefully up the harbor of New York, you knew she had spirit. She was salt-stained, and she was blotched with ugly patches of rust where her paint had scraped bare. But she rode high and straight, and her wind-whipped flags and pennants were crisp and bright in their colors. As I watched her draw near, she turned slightly to port, kicking up spray in the sunlight, and then she moved without hesitation to

31

her appointed place off Staten Island. Her anchor splashed down and her chain rattled out and she went silent with a great sigh, as though tired but happy to be home again.

That's what she should have been, tired but happy. She had just spent six months of hard living, traveling all the way to Murmansk and back.

I went aboard that afternoon to walk about and get to know her, for I felt we were going to be together for a long time. I liked what I saw, and I felt from the gentle rise and fall of her deck that she was the sort who would accept a strong attachment and give generously of herself.

She was a long, strong tanker of over ten thousand tons, stretching more than five hundred feet from bow to stern. She was no youngster, but her makers had seen to it that the good health of her youth would never desert her. She had been built in a Clyde River shipyard, which meant that she had been made by true craftsmen, the best in all the world.

She was designed to ride great waters and deep oceans and to withstand mighty storms. She also was designed for comfort, to bend and give with the tall waves, not to slam down and break her back against them. There was fine, rich wood in her panelings and pure bright brass in her fittings. Her stack rose higher than the stacks of younger tankers, and this might have made her look awkward to some observers. Personally I thought it added distinction and dignity to her appearance.

Her Murmansk experience had done her no good, of course. She showed the deep scars of shrapnel wounds and other marks of battle. She was in desperate need of facial surgery and something new to wear on her skin.

We took her around to the shipyard at Mariners Harbor, where they pulled her out of the water and went over her from top to bottom, bridge to keel, stem to rudder, fixing up all that needed to be fixed, and she never once complained.

Then they dressed her up in a brand new coat of gray paint and guided her back into the water again, and the familiar touch of the sea against her sides seemed to make her quiver with pleasure. She no longer looked worn out and weary. In her new skin of paint, she looked exactly like what she was, a restless lady with many places to go and many things to do.

I felt glad of the chance to move in and to go seeking those places with her, wherever they might be.

When we finally did go off together, after days of loading ammunition and stores and 100,000 barrels of petroleum, it was on a dark, cold morning, barely three hours after midnight.

We moved down the channel from Stapleton, forty-five ships in single file, like forty-five shadowy ghosts slipping quietly out of town; we passed the Staten Island watch station, glided through the gates of the submarine nets, took a last look astern at the dim lights of New York, and headed out to the gently rolling sea. We were beginning a lasting romance, *Gulfwing* and I—at times a perilous one, at times a frightening one, but always a lasting one. And that's the only kind of romance to have with any ship.

Later in the war, when the tide of battle had turned against the submarines, I spent many months riding a Liberty freighter, sometimes on the same sea lanes I had followed with *Gulfwing*. But the feeling of contentment was never quite the same. Nobody with even the lowest of morals and sensitivities could be so crude as to have a love affair with a Liberty ship.

They were big and useful and, for the most part, I must admit, they did the job they were built to do, carrying millions of tons of war supplies across the oceans and occasionally bringing back war prisoners. But they had no soul, no spirit, no sex appeal.

Also, they had a tendency to break apart.

This, I discovered, was because they were so hastily built and then so heavily loaded that they never were able to bend with the waves as my *Gulfwing* did. Instead, they stayed as rigid as a stick of wood, even in the mountainous seas of an arctic hurricane. And since what cannot bend must break, they developed an all-ocean epidemic of broken backs.

Mine broke apart once, ripping open just forward of the bridge in a jagged crack that ran amidships from port to starboard and five feet down the hull on either side. We were inbound for New York at the time, with only two days to go in calm weather, so there was no real danger involved. Nor was there any excitement ashore over our damage. When we crawled into port, the shipyard workers were noncommittal, as though Liberty ships with broken backs arrived as regularly as sundown. They said nothing but just welded a bulging seam over the cracked plates and sent us back into convoy. Liberty ships were expendable.

But ships like my *Gulfwing* were not. She was made for affection, and for the feel of knowing hands.

In all the time I spent with her, only once did I mistreat her, and then it was not done intentionally.

It happened in our first battle together, the first time I fired her stern gun.

She carried a good, reliable 3″/50 gun in her bow and eight 20-millimeter guns elsewhere, just as did most of the other ships in convoy. But mounted on her stern she carried a monstrous 5″/50 bag gun, a relic of old days and old wars, and possibly the only such ancient ramrod weapon assigned to any Armed Guard commander afloat.

Evidently the monster gun had never been fired since becoming a part of the *Gulfwing*. If it had been, somebody certainly would have printed a warning sign and hung it on the weapon's barrel, for when it went off it did so with disastrous results.

My idea in using it had been to score a hit with a heavy shell on the conning tower of a submarine some 4,000 yards behind the convoy. Whether we hit the submarine or not we never knew, for the instant the gun fired we were all too busy grappling with our own wreckage and testing our arms and legs for broken bones.

The weapon's thunderous concussion tore down stanchions, smashed the glass on the engine room telegraph dials, shattered a clock in the galley, blew radiator pipes from their fittings, broke shaving lotion bottles in five cabins, smashed ten drinking glasses in the saloon, splintered the carpenter's work bench, knocked out two door panels, ripped the door off the galley stove, and blew four pies out of the oven. But *Gulfwing*, I'm sure, forgave me. She was that kind of a lady—a lady with style, class, grace, warmth of heart, a touch of poetry, and a forgiving sense of humor.

Even now, after all this time, when I hear the sound of the wind on the sea at night, I miss her.

CHAPTER FOUR

NATIONS ON BOARD

ONE NIGHT IN A LITTLE FRENCH SEACOAST TOWN, sitting late over wine with the skipper of a heavy cruiser, I spent an hour or so listening to his tales of battle and his memories of moments of glory. And I found my thoughts wandering as he talked. But that was his fault for he unknowingly started them down other paths when he stared at his glass and said pensively:

"We pretend to hate war, and as civilized men we should. But we hold a secret in our hearts. Secretly we believe that a man is never so much a man as when he's a man at war."

Whether that sentiment or others made up the incentive, the manning of the convoy ships of the early 1940's produced a polyglot crowd of seamen and a motley set of excuses for their being there. Some said they had been lured aboard ship by the merchant marine bonus money; some explained that they hoped to avenge the death of a friend or a brother killed in an earlier battle; some simply shrugged that it was better to go to sea and eat good food than to be drafted into the Army and die in the mud; some considered the war an excellent opportunity for professional advancement; some gloated that it gave them a chance to get away from tiresome wives; and

36

only a few attributed their presence to patriotism.

Those of us in the Armed Guard sailed with the men of many nations, all of whom had been scooped up in the hungry manpower dragnet that built a prewar merchant marine of 50,000 men into a force of more than 200,000. It was a dragnet that was interested only in bodies, not in personalities.

As *Gulfwing* and I began our first voyage together, slipping out to sea in the harbor darkness, the men who walked the decks or who slumbered in their bunks below were from Egypt, Sweden, Norway, Latvia, Brazil, Puerto Rico, China, Romania, the Philippines, England, Ireland, Greece, and various corners of the United States. *Gulfwing* was no more than a typical ship in a typical convoy.

They were a strange lot, those men of the wartime merchant service. Sometimes they were brave, sometimes cowardly, sometimes savage, sometimes pitiable.

Sometimes they were men like Ivar, one of our mates, a Norwegian who came from Narvik but who never expected to see his home again. He talked to me about it one morning, just before first light. He was a tall, slender Scandinavian, soft-spoken and well-mannered. He loved the sea so deeply that he never went directly below when his watch relief arrived on the bridge. Instead, he would move just a few feet away from his station and spend the next half-hour or so in the open breeze, happy to be relieved of responsibility and content to relax and stare out across the moving waters. He had survived three ship-sinkings in the first five months of the war.

"But I would not be happy on land," he said, as we leaned on the rail and sipped coffee and watched the tumbling waves. "Not while the war is going on. When there is a war, a man's place is at sea. In peacetime it gets lonely and tiresome out here, and you feel lazy because there is never enough to do. But to be at sea in wartime makes you feel stronger and braver than you really are. And besides, when I am allowed to use one of your guns, perhaps I can kill a German. They killed my family and destroyed my home in Narvik, and the Japanese fliers killed my brother when he went with the Marines to Guadalcanal. Now I am the only one left, and this is the best place for me to be, out here where the enemy is hiding."

Ivar and I crossed the North Atlantic six times together. We drank a lot of ale in Bristol Channel pubs, and did some bad singing together as we groped through the blackouts on our way back to ship. We got to be good friends. In time he became as capable as any Navy gunner on the 20-millimeter Oerlikons and I used him in several fights, so somewhere along the line he may have killed his German without either of us knowing it. In convoy battles, it was always difficult to tell who did the killing.

He never lived to get back to Narvik to see what was left of his home. After risking his life over and over again at sea, it was ironic that he chose the wrong night between voyages to go alone to a waterfront saloon in Philadelphia. He was mugged and robbed there, and then he was beaten to death and his body was left in a dark alley.

Then there was Julio, the chicken farmer from Brazil, the plump and vulnerable answer to a card sharp's nightly prayer. He was a happy little fat man when he first came aboard in New York, and what kept him happy on his first voyage out was that he was sailing with a new group

of shipmates who had never before heard him boast about
the farm he owned on the outskirts of Recife. His favorite
relaxation, therefore, was to come off watch from the
engine room, head straight for the ship's saloon and the
coffee mess, and sit there talking endless farm-talk to
whomever might listen.

"It is a good farm, that one of mine," he would say
with a moonfaced smile. "When there was peace, I would
save my money from every voyage. No drinks, no women,
just always saving everything. And I would go home and
buy more land and go to sea again and save still more
money for still more land. I built a house there for my
wife Maria, and she stay happy there with the children.
I plant, I buy chickens, I plant more, I buy more chickens, I buy more land—after every voyage, something. We
make a very wonderful farm.

"Then we have this war come along. I tell my wife,
'Maria, they pay very wonderful money for ship's engi-
neers in war, and they say the black market is like a gold
mine. So you and the children take care of the farm while
I go to the war and get the dollars.' But she say, 'Julio,
forget the dollars and stay on the farm. You just want the
excitement. Stay where you belong and where you are
safe and where we need you.' But I came to the war
anyhow, and I used the bonus money in the black market,
and now I have many more dollars. And after I sail just
one more time, I will take them all home with me to buy
more land and more chickens. Women know nothing
about war when they say we just want the excitement!"

So Julio sailed with us, and it was supposed to be just
over and back, twice across the Atlantic, a round-trip
convoy on the New York-Liverpool run.

It might well have ended with that, except for the marathon poker game that went on in the ship's paint locker. That was a game that never stopped except when the ship was under attack. It ran twenty-four hours a day and built gigantic pots, as men coming off watch replaced men going on watch, and as men just waking up replaced men in need of sleep. It had been running for two months when Julio walked in on it one morning, saying he just wanted to watch and kibitz, then saying he just wanted to play a few hands in place of one of the regulars who was sitting out to get a haircut.

The other players welcomed him, moved over, and dealt him in. They had been waiting.

By the time the ship got back to New York on that voyage, Julio had lost more than $5,000. He signed on for another round-trip convoy, hoping to win his money back. At the end of that voyage, he was just about stripped of ready cash. He disappeared for forty-eight hours in New York, then returned to ship with a fresh roll of money. Before the next voyage was half over, he was selling bits and pieces of his farm in order to stay in the game. When finally we sailed back to the States once more, and tied up in Boston harbor to await orders, Julio was no longer a working poker player. He had become just another hanger-on in the paint locker, just another bystander without a dime to his name. Even his wages for the crossing had been mortgaged to the poker pot.

Again he signed on for one more voyage, but this time he did not sail. Instead, he left ship just before departure time without saying a word to anyone, and walked quietly down the gangplank and disappeared into the roaring waterfront traffic of Atlantic Avenue. He didn't even carry his suitcase ashore with him; he had gambled that away along with everything else.

Sometimes there were men aboard like Martinez, the little Filipino mess boy, who shared the dream of all the thousands of other little Filipino mess boys who ever went to sea—the dream of returning some day to his home in the islands and owning a gaudy restaurant in Manila. But to do that, two things were necessary: to make money and to stay alive.

Making money was easy. For being a mess boy, Martinez made more money than I did for being a Navy gunnery officer. He got paid $170 a month, plus $125 bonus for each Atlantic crossing, plus $5 daily for each day in the Mediterranean or on the Murmansk run, plus overtime wages for Sundays and holidays and after-hours, plus $125 for every air raid while in port—all this and no expenses to worry about. In itself it wasn't much of a fortune, perhaps, but it was an excellent working stake for the black market, for buying American cigarettes, stockings, and chocolate bars and peddling them in foreign ports at eight to ten times their cost. And that's where the profits grew thick. Martinez made all the money he needed, and banked it after every voyage.

Staying alive was a much more precarious problem. In Martinez' case, I'm certain, his fear helped him to live. He was never afraid of the submarines, but he was in deadly terror of the air raids, and this terror somehow gave him an uncanny sense of hearing, an ability to detect ominous sounds in the sky at night when nobody else could hear them. At one time, when the *Luftwaffe* blitzed London in February, 1944, we were tied up at the Royal Albert Docks for ten consecutive nights of bombings, and it was during this time that I discovered that Martinez could hear enemy planes approaching up the Thames Estuary long before the London sirens gave the alarm.

He would stand beside me on the bridge, looking off through the darkness toward the looming shadows of Woolwich Arsenal and Aldgate East, and occasionally cocking his head attentively in the direction of Margate and the Channel ports. I would hear nothing but the slurp of the tide, the creak of the lines, the fluttering wings of a night bird as it flew across our foredeck. Together Martinez and I would watch the clouds scud across the moon and feel the cold, damp river vapors chilling our cheeks. Sooner or later, he would start to tremble a little and would speak softly.

"They coming now, Lieutenant. I hear them coming. They very many this time."

Silence. I'd strain my ears but hear only the normal sounds of night.

"They coming, Lieutenant. I go now?"

"Go ahead, Martinez. Go below and stay there."

"Thank you, Lieutenant."

Quietly but swiftly, he would leave the bridge and pad across the deck and disappear below, anxious to put on his helmet and crawl into bed and pull a pillow over his face, for that was his way of living through an air raid's terror.

As soon as he had gone, I would pass the word to my gun crew, and moments later they would all be on station, waiting and tense in the darkness, but hearing no sound of the enemy. Then, after still more moments passed by, suddenly we would hear the first sound of the sirens, faint and far distant, wailing their shivery alarm from far down the Thames, relaying the warning up-river mile by mile, until at last all the sirens of London's dockside would be screaming their banshee howls and the glaring search-lights would explode their beams against the sky and the roar of Nazi bombers would make a hell of the heavens above.

I never knew Martinez to call it wrong. His ears were as sharply attuned to danger as the perfect radar of a bat. That, probably more than anything else, helped him to live through the war.

There were such men on the convoy ships. And there were men, too, such as Pete the Latvian, who was also re-markable for his ears but in a way quite unlike Martinez'. Nobody had paid any particular attention to Pete's ears until one night when he took shore liberty alone in Port Said; after that, nobody had the chance to notice them because when he returned to ship his ears were missing. Pete had done something offensive in a native dive, and a group of Egyptians had cut off his ears to remind him to behave.

There were men, too, like Hartley, the sensitive stew-ard, who dreamed hopefully of becoming a Broadway choreographer after the war. He occasionally practiced dance routines out on deck, and his reaction whenever anybody criticized his dinner menu was to stamp his foot and shout: "I think you're fresh!"

By contrast, there was another steward who sailed with us long after Hartley had decided to stay on shore. He was sad-faced and bald-headed, this man, and he carried himself erect and proud, and his name was Karl.

Karl was born in Bratislava, of a wealthy Austrian family, back in the far-gone days of Austrian imperial glory. He was graduated from the Vienna Military Academy in 1909, and became a lieutenant in the Royal Austrian Artillery under Emperor Franz Josef.

In World War I, he fought at the front for forty-four months, and saw his father and three brothers killed.

In November, 1916, when Franz Josef died of a fever at Schönbrunn Castle, Karl was one of twenty outstanding officers selected from the entire Austrian Army to escort the Emperor's body to its tomb. By the time the war ended, he had been decorated fourteen times for outstanding bravery under fire.

Karl left Austria in 1919 to travel to the United States. He spent the next eight years as an artillery sergeant in the United States Army, serving in China, Latin America, and the Philippine Islands. In 1927, with what he had saved and what he could borrow, he opened a small butcher shop in New York, and began to put aside the profits that eventually made him a wealthy man.

He never returned to Austria, but he never forgot it either. He sat in my cabin one night, with his old decorations and his old photographs spread out on a blanket in front of him, and told me stories of what old Vienna had been like in the days of Franz Josef, and he wept unashamedly for the passing of a world that could never return.

There were such men. And then there were rheumatic old ship captains, recalled from retirement, who never left their cabins from the start of a voyage to its end. And there were young captains, pushed up to the responsibility of command years before their time, who never left the bridge. There were the frightened men like Stanley, the Polish quartermaster, who fainted at the wheel one sunny afternoon off Greenland at the mere sight of a periscope rising from the sea. And there were the brave ones like Jan, the Romanian, who dove overboard after a drowning friend and got snatched from the waves by the crew of a Japanese submarine; they lashed him to the conning tower in a tangle of barbed wire; then they left him there, went below, and put the submarine into a dive.

Such were the men of the merchant marine, in those early days of the convoy ships. Such were the men already aboard *Gulfwing* when I joined her with a crew of twenty-two Armed Guard gunners and one Navy signalman, most of whom had never sailed beyond sight of land.

"The Armed Guards," a Hearst Syndicate columnist wrote about that time, "haven't had as much publicity as the average two-headed calf gets. But those close to the sea know the tremendous role they are playing in keeping the Allied lifeline unbroken.

"They don't sail on battlewagons, destroyers, or cruisers but on tankers, Liberty ships, and freighters. There is no glamor in their job. It is rough, mean, and hazardous. It is their responsibility, with antiaircraft and heavier guns, to get their ship and its precious cargo through subs and dive bombers and torpedo planes. They are the last to leave the ship in case of disaster.

"But no branch of the Navy has a finer spirit. The boys average eighteen or nineteen years of age, and most of them never saw the sea before they sailed in convoy as fighting men. They come from the plains of Kansas, the hills of Kentucky, and the forests of Oregon.

"They are doing just about the toughest job in the Navy."

I was to find as the months went by that this was a

fair appraisal. From my oldest Navy gunner, who was forty-five and the father of six children, to my youngest, who had faked his age and was only fifteen, they took to the ocean like the offspring of a porpoise, and they took to their weapons like a backwoodsman takes to his squirrel gun.

Weeks after we had been together—after hurricanes and ice storms, after bombs and torpedoes, after flame and flying steel—I wrote about them in a private journal, with an entry that read:

"*Monday*—Another day of hot sun, bright skies, and a dead flat ocean. This is unbelievable, that we can be going through such beautiful weather at this particular point. We are squarely in the middle of where the fog belt should be, in the very place where we lost contact with our convoy for three days and nights on the last crossing and where, on every crossing, we have had to grope along blindly through thick banks of fog, sometimes unable even to see the bow of our own ship.

"But all day long now, we've sailed beneath a brassy sun.

"The new Second Mate has been sailing back and forth across this same North Atlantic zone for twenty years, and he says he has never seen anything like this before. But we enjoy it, even though the book says it cannot possibly be happening.

"This afternoon, with time being heavy, I killed an hour or two trying to find out just exactly what my average Navy gunner is like. And the result sounds like standard material for another chorus of 'Ballad for Americans.'

"Using the statistical information in their records, plus

what I know about them personally, I find the composite gunner to be just over nineteen years old, with two years of high school education. At his worst, he quit school in the Fourth Grade. (How did that one get into the Navy?) At his best, he spent two years in college and plans to go back for his degree when the war ends.

"He has been in the Navy for ten months. He despises the British sailors. He has a girl back home to whom he writes very terrible love letters (and I'm very tired of censoring them). If he has to leave the Atlantic, he would prefer not to go home but would like to get into the Pacific Fleet and start fighting the Japanese.

"His heritage links, I find, are nine parts English, four parts German, three parts Irish, three parts French, two parts Italian, and one part each of Romanian, Czech, Swedish, Dutch, Polish, Jewish, Bohemian, French-Canadian, and Penobscot Indian.

"When it comes to religion, he is fourteen parts Roman Catholic, eleven parts Episcopalian, four parts Baptist, one part Lutheran, one Methodist, one Jewish.

"His home is in Georgia, Florida, Michigan, New York (3), Massachusetts (4), Rhode Island (3), Connecticut (2), Pennsylvania (5), Missouri (2), Delaware, Tennessee, Iowa, California, Wisconsin, Virginia, Mississippi, Indiana, New Jersey, and North Dakota.

"When the war came along, he was a truck driver, bricklayer, well-driller, lathe scraper, shipyard worker, railroad section hand, post office clerk, precision grinder, grocery store manager, stock clerk, student, farmer, carpenter, welder, office boy, machinist, fireman, optical worker, dairyman, steel mill laborer, and mortician's helper.

"In two cases he is married, in thirty he is single.

"He got his boot training at Newport, Norfolk, Little Creek, Great Lakes, San Diego, Chicago, Sampson, Gulfport, Noroton Heights, Conn., and Auburn, Ala.

"He likes dogs, cares nothing about money except to spend it, wouldn't be in the Army or the Merchant Marine for ten times what little he's making out here, and thinks the English girls are cold and stupid.

"He enjoys sailing in stormy weather. He enjoys the excitement of attack alarms, the sound of battle, the firing of the guns. He does not like to make up his bunk, and he has to be nagged by his petty officers to keep his shirt tails tucked inside his pants.

"When he writes a letter home, he does it in about three paragraphs that say nothing, and then he winds it up by saying, 'Well, as there is nothing more to say, I will close now. Good bye.' When he writes to his girl, he tells incredible and overpowering lies about all the brave things he's doing in the war, and he hints clumsily that he's going to ask her to marry him as soon as he gets back.

"If he gets a change of duty, he would like to go from the Armed Guard to Destroyer Escorts, but he would prefer to stay in the Armed Guard for the rest of the war if the Navy would let him.

"I have known him to eat ten eggs for breakfast, six pork chops for lunch, and a full pound of steak for dinner. Not often, but it has happened.

"He does not complain about the conditions under which he has to work and fight. And out of the hundreds of orders given him, he has never once asked, 'Why?' or hesitated an instant in carrying them out.

"He likes to take over the wheel and steer the ship and leave a straight wake. Next to that, he likes to loaf on deck with a record player and listen to the songs of Bing Crosby.

"He enjoys long discussions and arguments about such weighty subjects as battle tactics, Naval history, dictatorships, women, and God—but in port, he has been known to spend $5.25 at one whack for 'Superman' and other comics and come back to ship bragging about the fact that the clerk tossed in two extra copies in return for such a fine order.

"His niche in the Navy is somewhere between John Paul Jones and Alfred, the cartoon character in *Collier's* magazine. Wherever it is, he fills it well and does his job the way it's supposed to be done."

Oddly enough, the composite Navy gunner and the average merchant mariner got along like old members of the same neighborhood gang.

This (although they probably would have denied it) was because they shared two emotions, a love for the sea and a liking for combat.

And, too, it was because they were shipmates, regardless of uniform, regardless of background, regardless of hopes and fears.

As an old Navy officer, who loved both merchant ships and warships, once expressed it:

"The sea demands more of men, but it gives more. No one who knows the meaning of the word 'shipmate' can fail to understand what it is that the sea gives, that the land can never give—the feeling of standing and working together, of individual strength and energy being pooled together for the safety and welfare of all, the sense of one's only antagonist being the elements that surround him."

CHAPTER FIVE

SHIP PERSONALITIES

A SHIP CAN BE TIMID OR COLD, BRUTAL OR COMPASSION-ate, cowardly or heroic, with a personality just as distinctive as that of any man or woman.

I do not mean that a ship, in her behavior, merely reflects the peculiar characteristics of the men who sail her. She does more than that; she draws out their personalities and blends them until they become a whole thing, and then she absorbs that whole thing into herself and makes of it her own personality. For better or worse, that is when she comes alive. From then on, she is an individual with a heart and a soul of her own.

One time, for example, when we were at anchor off Bangor in Belfast Lough, awaiting a convoy rendezvous, we spent a day or two close abeam of the British cruiser, H.M.S. *Glasgow*. Under moonlight or midday sun, *Glasgow* had an air about her that marked her as slovenly, unkempt, and fatigued. If she had been a woman, she would have been the kind of a woman whose stockings always droop and show runs, and whose hair is always dirty and stringy, no matter if she has just had a shampoo. Line for line and point for point, she should have been one of the trimmest ships in the Royal Navy, for she was barely six years old and had been designed as one of a graceful 9,100-ton cruiser class. She should have carried her twelve 6-inch guns with a heroic air. But for some reason she could not. Something, at some time, had gone out of her heart, and no matter how you looked at her she always seemed to be sulking and feeling sorry for herself.

On the other hand, I remember with affection and admiration another British ship, the *Empire Emerald,* our companion on many a convoy crossing. Here was a lady of the seas who had everything going against her, for she was nothing but a small merchant tanker and she was assigned to some of the most dangerous and dirtiest work on the North Atlantic and Murmansk runs. Yet through it all, she sailed her course with an air of class and grace, and unmistakable sex appeal.

Glasgow made you know, without looking, that there would be garbage and galley soot on her decks. *Emerald,* with her low-cut stack and her proud bow, somehow reminded you of a lady who had gone through an exhausting day but who now, in the evening, had showered and touched up her fingernails and was determined to get out of her apartment and enjoy a date for cocktails and dinner.

In convoy, *Emerald* almost always drew a position as a column leader, and it was good to see her there. By *Gulfwing's* standards, she was not heavily armed but, nevertheless, she carried about her an air of confidence that was caught up and displayed by other ships in her company. Whenever the submarines came, she was a graceful thing to watch, leading her column into emergency turns of forty-five degrees to port or starboard, almost as though she were gliding into an exclusive yacht basin rather than maneuvering on the war-strewn waves of a treacherous sea.

The distinctive thing between *Glasgow* and *Empire Emerald,* was the difference in their personalities, and the fact that one was indolent while the other was always poised and proud.

It was a quirk of personality, too, that made *Clan MacArthur* a memorable ship, for she was beyond any question one of the most pathetically timid vessels ever to sail in a North Atlantic convoy.

We first crossed with *Clan MacArthur* on a voyage that cleared New York at 4 o'clock one dark morning in the spring of 1943. We were bound for the United Kingdom, in a 54-ship convoy that formed up at sea in a pattern nine columns wide. We were to be joined off Nova Scotia by another fifteen ships coming out from Halifax, and then we were to head across the North Atlantic in a twelve-column spread, with a British destroyer and three little Canadian corvettes along to provide us with escort protection.

We were only four days out when the weather turned bad. The wind had been whining and rising all afternoon, and before nightfall it had whipped up formidable strength. The waves grew higher and more savage with every hour. There never was any sunset that evening, just a melancholy disappearance into gray, rain-streaked clouds.

By four-thirty the following morning, the North Atlantic was at its dirtiest, meanest, and most treacherous. Tremendous black waves crashed down on *Gulfwing's* decks, sending spray far above the flying bridge and making the whole convoy toss and roll and sideslip like a fleet of cork boats stirred by the hand of a demented giant.

Before going out on deck that day, I dressed for the

foul weather in long woolen underwear, knee length woolen socks, overshoes, heavy pants, sweat shirt, a Navy turtleneck sweater, waterproof jacket, rubber windbreaker, leather mittens, and oilskins with a parka hood.

Looking back on it now, that seems like excessive clothing for a morning in May, but the North Atlantic has never learned to respect seasonal traditions of style in dress. In fact, I remember adding a sheepskin coat and an arctic face mask to the outfit when the storm abruptly changed from a pounding rain to a lashing gale of sleet.

It was impossible to keep men on the bow and stern guns that morning, for *Gulfwing's* decks were awash most of the time.

Our position in the convoy was in station 93, the third ship down from the leader in the ninth column. Behind us, in station 94, rode *Clan MacArthur*, a bulky, black, British freighter with a clumsy high bow. She had been there astern of us ever since leaving New York. Apparently, though, she was in constant dread of getting lost or of sliding out of station, for she had been asking us repeatedly by blinker signal: "What is your number, please?" That had been going on for three days, and had become dully irritating.

Now, as the dawn darkness gave way to a wet gray morning, *Clan MacArthur* once again picked up her nervous blinking. This time, though, we were too busy to reply to her immediately. At the moment, we were talking by blinker light to another ship that had caught our attention from three columns away and that was asking us to relay an emergency message from her to the Convoy Commodore.

She was an American freighter, the *Aedamus Burke*.

According to our convoy chart, she was bound for Liverpool with a cargo of sulphur and explosives. Now, suddenly, that chart was out of date; she would not be making the journey.

"We have split our main boiler," came the message that glimmered across the waves. "We must drop out and turn back. Please pass the news to the Commodore. We wish you a successful voyage and a safe return."

And with that, she swung heavily out of column, labored around in a turmoil of seas, and finally started slowly back toward Nova Scotia, a lonely, crippled ship in perilous submarine waters.

"Good-bye and good luck," we blinked after her, and then we turned to acknowledge the frantic signal lights that were coming to us through the storm from the bridge of *Clan MacArthur.*

"What is your number, please?" she queried.

"The same as yesterday," we told her. "You are right where you belong."

The storm grew worse as the day dragged along. It broke the pipes of our heating system and turned our cabins into drafty freezers. It hurled its waves so high that the sea ran under the bulkheads and left cold, sloshing torrents along the passageways. It threw hundreds of fish upon the decks, and washed them away again, and then threw up hundreds more.

That night the storm moved away, the fog closed in, and we lost the convoy.

We did not realize what had happened until just before dawn the next day, when *Clan MacArthur* sent a nervous blinker signal toward us through a break in the wet murk.

"Where are the other ships?" she wanted to know.

Sure enough, when the fog lifted again for a moment or two, we could see that they were gone.

"Follow us," we told *Clan MacArthur,* though we had no idea where we were going.

She was as obedient as a dog on a leash. She followed us so closely for the rest of the day that at times she seemed ready to come aboard and sit on our stern and have coffee. As the long hours went by, the weather stayed dirty—too dirty for us to see where we were going or what might be coming toward us. Through thick fog, snow squalls, gusts of sleet and rain, hour after hour we plunged blindly ahead. And, occasionally, we would see a flicker of light from *Clan MacArthur's* signal bridge. It was always the same appeal:

"What is your number, please?"

At last the wind dropped and the seas calmed down to a long, gentle roll, and we rigged a fog buoy and strung it out astern for *Clan MacArthur* to follow. Under murky conditions, a fog buoy was a great help to convoy ships that were trying to keep their place in column and that were constantly in danger of being overrun by a ship astern, or of running up too close on the ship ahead. It was nothing but a sparlike apparatus attached to a wire cable, but as it spun out and got dragged along at the end of its towline, it churned up its own splashing wake. This gave the lookouts on the ship astern something positive by which to guide. It assured them that all was well with the ship ahead, even though they could not see her through the thick, intervening wall of fog.

We had scarcely put our fog buoy into operation before *Clan MacArthur* sent up a wail on her whistle and came wallowing out of the mist to plunge alongside, beam to beam, running so close we could hear her plates creaking in the strain of the waves.

She blinked at us jerkily. We bellowed across the water at her: "Sheer off! Get back in station."

"Periscope!" somebody yelled from her bridge. "Periscope astern of you! Open fire."

"That's our fog buoy!" we shouted back. "Return to your station."

She slipped back almost reluctantly, like a timid child being sent to its darkened bedroom. A few minutes later, she was blinking at us through the mist again:

"Thank you for the fog buoy. Much better now. Will keep watch for submarines astern of both of us."

The fog lasted for another forty-eight hours, wrapping us in a blind chill and making it impossible to see beyond our own deck-length world. Occasionally, somewhere out in the gray curtain that hid the sea, we would hear the whistle of some other lost ship, mournfully blowing its station number in Morse code, as though sending out an appeal for some other member of its column to make itself known and join company. We would respond with our own station number, blowing the call that meant "93," and *Clan MacArthur* would pick it up by blowing "94," as though we had any doubt that she was still back there. Then the silence would fold in again, silence except for the trembling rumble of *Gulfwing's* engines and the splashing of the waves along her hull and the drip-drip-drip of fog moisture falling from her plates to her deck.

Finally, just before evening, the fog thinned again and visibility opened, and we could identify other ships that were scattered across the heaving seas.

Of the original sixty-nine that had been together when last the sun was shining, only twenty-seven were left. But that was enough to assure us that there would be many others, somewhere below the horizon, and that most of us would be back in formation by the time we reached our next midocean rendezvous point at noon the next day.

Clan MacArthur still clung to us, except for one brief moment of desertion. That happened the next morning, when most of us were back in formation again, and when suddenly our fog buoy snapped its cable and drifted back and out of sight.

We didn't care, for visibility was good by then. But *Clan MacArthur* wasn't happy about it. Twice she pulled alongside with her blinker light flashing and notified us: "Your fog buoy is missing, old man."

"Not needed," we replied. "Return to your station."

She dropped back unwillingly, staying much closer to our stern than was necessary. Then suddenly, to our astonishment, she swung out of line to port and churned hurriedly over to the next column and took up a position astern of the last ship there.

We watched her through the glasses, and finally saw the reason for her strange move. The last ship in Column Eight also had strung a fog buoy. *Clan MacArthur* had spotted it and was not going to let it go to waste.

Nor were we going to let any other column take away our pet. We hurriedly rigged a temporary fog buoy by lashing an empty oil drum to a length of cable and dropping it astern. And it worked like magic. No sooner had it started to send up its spray than *Clan MacArthur* swerved out of her new position and hurried back to where she belonged, as close to our guide line as she could get.

Then, just before darkness fell, she blinked at us with her signal lamp once more.

"Thanks for the buoy, old man."

"Happy to help," we replied.

She still had one more point to make: "If the weather gets sticky tonight, will you please light a light that we can follow."

There was no point in acknowledging that message. If we had turned on a night light in those waters, one of our escort ships would have moved in and shot it out without hesitation. I have always wondered how *Clan Mac-Arthur,* with her timidity complex, would have reacted to the sound of shellfire close aboard after dark.

But the nervous ones and the proud ones and the slovenly ones were not the only types of ships in the early convoys. There were also the happy ones, the embarrassed ones, and even the bawdy ones.

We crossed once with a ship that was truly happy— as happy as children at recess or at a May Basket party. And that was because she had taken on the personalities of the youngsters who were aboard.

She was a Dutch ship, proudly flying the flag of the lost Netherlands and manned entirely by Dutch seamen. What's more, they had their families aboard, probably because they no longer had homes of their own on shore, since the German armies had long ago overrun their nation.

But though they had been stricken by the fortunes of war, they never showed it. As we watched them through the binoculars, day in and day out, we came to know their routine. Each sunny morning, they would all turn to, children and mothers alike, and scrub their ship until it fairly glistened. After breakfast, they would all take a brisk walk, four times around the deck. Then it was time for school, with the children sitting in separated groups around their teachers, and holding their books, and standing up to recite their lessons; they even had blackboards, propped incongruously against gun mounts and cargo crates. And at recess time, what with games and races, the ship looked for all the world like a floating playground.

Happiness was the personality of that Dutch ship—happiness and love of family—and it somehow spread to other ships in the convoy, and made us all feel glad to be where we were, and doing what we were doing.

Another time, we were in convoy with a ship that fairly dripped with embarrassment and self-consciousness. This was probably a personality trait that was acquired through a single unfortunate incident, for there had been nothing to distinguish the ship at the start of the voyage aside from the fact that she was a Norwegian freighter, no longer with a true home port of her own.

Her trouble came without warning, midway on the crossing from New York to London. It came on a warm, sunshiny Sunday afternoon, when there were no submarine alerts on the signal boards and nothing to do but loaf away the lazy hours.

Rather than waste time, the gunners aboard the Norwegian turned out about midafternoon to clean all their weapons. One by one they went over them, with oil, grease, and rags, until they had worked their way from the foredeck all the way back aft to their stern gun, a menacing piece that looked like a 4″/50.

That's where they came to grief. Somebody had left a shell in the gun's breech. Somebody tripped the trigger. With a flash and a roar, a deadly projectile ripped its way down past the five ships in line astern of the Norwegian, screaming head-high over the decks and plunging into the sea with a mighty splash.

It was a miracle shot, a freak that caused no damage and injured no man. But it set off an indignant uproar of whistles and a frantic flashing of signal lamps from the Convoy Commodore's ship, and a foaming rush of escorts converging on the scene ready for battle.

All in an instant, the Norwegian took on a hang-dog personality that stayed with her through the rest of the voyage. From that moment on, she seemed to slink rather than sail, and there was something so apologetic about her that her crew seemed almost obsequious as they went about their duties on deck. After she left us in London, we never saw her again.

Then there was the bawdy one, the Russian ship with beefy Russian women working shoulder to shoulder with their men.

She traveled with us once from Halifax to northern Scotland, to the Loch Ewe rendezvous point where ships assembled for the long and dangerous run to Murmansk. And when she first fell into position, in the column station off our starboard beam, she seemed to give off an atmosphere reminiscent of the humor of raucous, backroom stag parties—of tin cans tied to the honeymoon automobile—of the big night at the lodge when the exotic blonde pops out of the cardboard cake.

We were three days out in company with that ship when we discovered that she did, in truth, live up to her personality.

It happened in the midmorning of a sunny day when work was slack and the sea was smooth. At a quiet hour like that, aboard any ship in any convoy, you could always find somebody whiling away the time by staring through binoculars at other ships in the convoy, to see what was going on among the neighbors. In that respect, convoy sailors as a whole were shameless Peeping Toms.

On this particular morning, I was standing beside the First Mate, drinking a cup of coffee, while we leaned against the rail on the starboard wing of the bridge and stared across at the Russians. The First Mate had the binoculars. Suddenly he started swinging his arm over his head.

"They're waving at us," he said. "Two of those Russian broads. Here, take a look."

He handed me the glasses. I put them in focus and looked across to see a duplicate version of what we were doing—one woman staring at us through the binoculars while the one beside her gave us an enthusiastic wave.

I picked up my coffee cup and held it high in a cordial salute.

The response was startling. The bigger of the two Russian women promptly unzipped the front of her blouse, reached inside, pulled out a mountainous right breast, and gaily waved it up and down. She had to use both hands.

The First Mate tossed her a farewell flip of his fingers and quietly turned away.

"If only they looked like women," he said regretfully.

CHAPTER SIX

ESCORTS AT WORK

SOMEWHERE, I SUPPOSE, A VALHALLA HAS LONG SINCE been prepared for the braver men who fought at sea in World War II. Or perhaps, instead, they will wait out their eternity where all good mariners go, in the cool and shadowy depths of Fiddler's Green.

But wherever their destiny may take them, there should be a special Hall of Valor set aside for the ones arriving from the convoy escort ships.

They were a distinctive breed of fighting sailors, and they shared with the Armed Guard gunners and the merchant marine seamen a kind of three-dimensional warfare that sometimes left them talking gibberish and striking out against shadows.

They fought an enemy who attacked from the air and from the surface of the sea and from the depths below, but that, of course, was to be expected of any Navy crew. Beyond that, though, were the deep scars caused by North Atlantic savagery, by having to fling a few tiny corvettes against a vast fleet of submarines, by doing battle among thundering icebergs one month and in the grip of a tropical hurricane the next, by trying to shepherd sprawling convoys across thousands of miles of sea without letting a single ship fall behind, by the terrible sight of helpless swimmers caught in the knives of a propeller, by the exhausting demands of endless patrols in the vast space between continents, by the frustration of having to keep pace with a slow, ten-knot convoy, by the stink of unchanged clothing, the cuts and fractures of storm wounds, the frightening hysteria of men gone berserk, the horrible sight of sailors being cremated in flaming oil, the loneliness, and the neglect.

Most of those men, in most of our convoys, were Canadian or British, and most of our escort ships were their own corvettes and destroyers. We came to know many of them well, for time after time the same little warships were assigned again and again to travel with us, and the sociable corvette that had been at our side off Iceland in the spring might show up to join us unannounced off East Africa in the fall.

We also felt a warm affection for their escort aircraft carriers because one of the first to go on convoy duty—if not the first one of all to fight in the North Atlantic— became a staunch companion of ours in a long, running battle against the submarines.

That happened in the early part of May, 1943, on the same convoy crossing that had brought us together with the timid *Clan MacArthur.*

Other escort carriers had been hunting German submarines in the North Atlantic for several weeks by that time, but without good results. Among them, the U.S.S. *Bogue* had sailed from Puget Sound six months earlier and had moved through the Panama Canal and then joined the Atlantic War in February; but not until May 23 did *Bogue* achieve the first positive submarine sinking scored by an American carrier.

Meanwhile, some two weeks earlier, we had emerged from a severe storm and had pulled together the remnants of a scattered, eastbound convoy and were entering the perilous midocean gap where the submarine wolf packs lurked and where land-based aircraft could not reach them. It was Friday, May 7. Within the next forty-eight hours, we were to welcome an escort carrier into our company for the first time. Within the next seven days, we were to chop apart and methodically destroy the heart of a huge U-boat wolf pack.

As the faded log recalls it:

"We changed course to the southeast just after midnight, and the fog was gone with the dawn. I left my cabin and went to the wheelhouse at 4 A.M. and found we were sailing a clear, smooth sea, and a red sun was just rising off our port bow.

"When daylight finally spread and the shadows were gone, the First Mate and I went up to the flying bridge to check the rest of the convoy and count the survivors of the storm. We could see thirty-four ships already in line and another six just coming over the horizon. A reconnaissance plane circled the convoy from afar out, staying too close to the horizon to show its identity, but letting us know that there was a warship somewhere nearby. We watched it with misgivings. All we could do was to hope that it was on our side, for our escort ships had vanished, scattered about for miles by the storm, or perhaps prowling around beyond our sight in search of stragglers. In any event, we were on our own, and it was a lonely feeling. Probably already we were being trailed and scouted by an unseen submarine.

"Late in the morning, an American aircraft carrier accompanied by three destroyers came foaming over the horizon and bore down upon us from the east. For a while we had the glorious feeling that this was to be our new escort. But we should have known better. The whole outfit sailed right on past us without so much as a blink of recognition, bound west toward home and leaving us feeling like unwanted children. In the middle of the afternoon, though, two Canadian destroyers and three corvettes came into sight and flashed us their recognition signals and steamed to meet us. They took up their stations ahead and along the flanks, and at last we were officially on our way again.

"By now we were forty ships, survivors of the original sixty-nine that had begun the voyage off Nova Scotia. The others had become lost, or had turned back, or perhaps in some cases had been sunk. We could not tell.

"The good weather was not long with us. All day the sea underwent a slow change from serenity to choppiness, then to roughness and, finally, at day's end, to wildness. Heavy rain squalls and gale winds hit us again, and as darkness came down the sleet began to fall.

"*Saturday, May 8*—As everyone aboard knows, this cannot go on much longer, this strange isolation from the submarines. Here we are, far out in the Atlantic, squarely in the middle of the 600-mile gap where the hunting is best, and yet we are being ignored as though we were phantoms. Our escort is pitifully small and poorly armed. Our ships are laden almost entirely with cargoes of gasoline, oil, and explosives that are badly needed on the other side. We are an ideal quarry, but there is no sign whatever of the enemy. It is too good to last, and it is very hard on the nerves, for as every hour goes by the inevitable working of the law of averages creeps closer.

"I am puzzled by what has happened to cause the change in our original convoy schedule, and so are the merchant officers. Nobody seems to know what's going on, and if the Convoy Commodore has any information he declines to share it with us.

"According to our New York plan, though, we should have been far up beyond Greenland's Cape Farewell by now, and instead we are skirting the Azores, many miles south of our outlined route. At this moment, we are heading straight toward Gibraltar, and instead of feeling the cold winds of the arctic on our faces we are moving toward the warm winds of Africa, and nobody can understand why we're here.

"If the original port schedule holds firm, with Britain as our destination, it means that we must turn soon to make our way in a northward climb within easy attack-range of the submarine pens of Lorient and St. Nazaire and the land-based *Luftwaffe* in France. And that will not be good.

"Two unidentified aircraft looked us over from the edge of the horizon at twilight. If they were friendly, they could have helped to ease our tension a little by approaching close enough to let us know. If they were unfriendly, they will have charted our position by now and relayed it to the submarines.

"*Sunday, May 9*—They were unfriendly. At 10:25 this morning, the Convoy Commodore jarred us into action by sending up the flag hoist alarm, *WF*—the two bright alphabet flags that mean, '*Enemy submarines at hand!*'

"Instantly a destroyer that had been refueling in mid-column dropped her pipe line and rushed off toward the north. The other escorts bit into the waves and went racing out from our flanks.

"The Commodore immediately sent up a second flag hoist, *E*—'*Emergency turn 45 degrees to starboard.*' As one ship, the whole convoy swung to right-oblique and moved into top speed.

"We manned our guns and stood by, watching the escorts drop their depth charges and feeling the pound of the concussion beneath our feet. Then, just as we completed our emergency turn, a wild squall came tearing across the sea and buried us so deep in rain, spray, and wet wind that we could scarcely make out the Commodore's flags. It was partly by guess and only partly by reading his signals that we were able, somehow, to go through an intricate series of zigzag turns, but we had the satisfaction of knowing, when the storm subsided two hours later, that it would have taken a genius of a submarine commander to have stayed with us.

"Our escorts came hustling back then, like hounds returning from a rabbit hunt. They took up their familiar patrol patterns, ahead and on the flanks, and dropped one corvette astern to guard us from the rear. For the moment, we felt safe. . . ."

But the submarines were somewhere around. Probably if any of us had been asked at that moment what we would rather see than any other object in the world, we would have spoken out unanimously for the sight of an escort aircraft carrier.

Then, suddenly, to our astonishment, there she came, a

British flattop where nobody had ever expected to see one, wallowing out of the gray spume that overhung the sea, bearing down across our course from the northeast, with three hardy-looking British destroyers foaming along in her company.

We watched her in silence, and perhaps it was a bitter sort of silence too, for it was scarcely two days since one of our own carriers and three destroyers had passed us by. Now we looked for the same treatment from the approaching British—and this time it would be worse, for we knew now that the submarines had found us and were waiting for the right moment to attack.

But as we stared in delighted disbelief, the carrier proved us wrong. She crossed our course, just as we had expected. Then, instead of showing us her wake, she turned and swung down along our port flank, and turned again as she drew astern of us. Then she stepped up her speed, quickly overtook us, and moved straight ahead into our convoy formation, where she nosed her way into a column position directly on *Gulfwing's* beam. And as she reduced her speed to keep pace with the convoy, she flashed us a one-word blinker message:

"Greetings."

As carriers go, she was an ungainly looking thing. Probably, in the shipyards of Scotland, she had started out to become a cruiser and then the Admiralty had decided to outfit her with a flight deck instead of gun turrets. And as planes go, hers were not the Grumman Wildcats or Avengers that you'd expect to see on a carrier; they were, in fact, old Swordfish biplanes, all twelve of them.

But she was such a comforting sight in convoy that no

one-word message was ever more sincere than the one we
flashed back in answer to her arrival:

"Welcome."

For the next five days and nights, with the carrier in
our midst, we fought a running battle with a wolf pack
of twenty-five submarines.

That first twilight after the coming of the carrier, the
Commodore sent up the familiar *WF* flag hoist again just
before darkness fell. The submarines stayed with us all
through the black hours, snapping at our flanks, and now
and then forcing us into emergency turns. But our escort
ships—five destroyers and three corvettes—managed to
hold them off and keep them at a safe distance. After a
shuddering depth charge barrage at 4:20 A.M., we were
able to eat breakfast in peace, enjoy the sunrise, and look
forward to getting a little sleep.

The Swordfish planes began taking off just after day-
break, and for hour after hour they flew their patrols and
kept the submarines submerged. They ran their air sweeps
far out ahead on our course, and out on our flanks and
astern of us.

It was not until early afternoon that the enemy finally
was able to slip in through the sweeps and come close
enough to start action.

Then at 2:35 P.M., four destroyers and one Swordfish
just ahead of the convoy flashed simultaneous alarms. The
Commodore ran up his flag hoists: *"Enemy submarines—
emergency turn to starboard."*

All over the convoy, alarm gongs rang, gun crews
leaped to action, ships heeled sharply, turning in tortured
wakes, merchant sailors jumped to their jobs as ammunition handlers, guns barked, depth charges churned the

sea and made it thunder. The lines and columns wheeled and dipped as though the tankers and freighters were dolphins at play. The sun glistened down on whitecaps, blue-green waves, and colored signal flags whipping in the wind. The Swordfish planes roared back and forth overhead.

And in the middle of the maelstrom, a gigantic whale belched to the surface just off *Gulfwing's* port bow, took a frantic look at the whole scene, and headed for the uncluttered waves astern at record speed.

By 4 o'clock, the submarines again had withdrawn and our ships returned to normal cruising. But this, we knew, would only be a temporary lull.

The Escort Commander aboard his destroyer knew it also, and as we stood on the bridge of *Gulfwing* and watched his ship at twilight, we saw him flash his signal lamp to the Convoy Commodore. His message read:

"Stay alert for any type of attack by air, surface, or submarine all night. Make no attempt to evacuate or scatter the convoy regardless of what happens. Stay with the escort and the escort will stay with you, whatever may come."

What came was a covering gale. An angry storm struck just after dark, piling the waves into turmoil and hiding the ships in a seething blackness. It was a protective tempest, and it stayed with us throughout the night.

But by dawn on Tuesday, the storm was gone and the sea and the sky were clear. Now it was time for the enemy to move in again.

Our Swordfish planes bombed two submarines that day. They destroyed one about two miles astern of the convoy shortly after 7 o'clock in the morning, and another off the starboard wing at sundown.

But in spite of that, it was not a happy day. Rather, it was a day of sadness for all of us in the convoy, for we learned to our sorrow that we had lost one of our Sword-fish pilots.

The news came in the form of a question that was blinked to *Gulfwing* from the carrier just after sunrise. It said:

"Please pass this query to the whole convoy. Has any ship any information to report on the fate of one of our planes that had to make a forced landing in the sea near convoy at 0200 this morning? Our other planes report no trace of wreckage or survivors."

The message contained its own answer, for at 0200 the all-night storm had been at its greatest peak of fury.

A little while later, the carrier sent up a flag hoist communique that, in those days, spelled out a message infinitely sad: "One of our aircraft is missing."

There was not a ship in the convoy that would not have dropped out of column and gladly risked a torpedo-ing, just for the chance to turn back in search of the missing flier. But the orders were to keep moving ahead at top speed, and so we left behind us a young man probably dead, but who if still alive might be alone on a tiny rubber raft, trying to persuade himself to be patient, telling himself that his friends would come to his rescue, that they certainly wouldn't abandon him and leave him alone to die.

At 9:20 that night, the submarines were back again. While the corvettes were dropping depth charges, our convoy altered course and headed due north, running directly parallel to the coast of France.

Next morning, the battle continued under a bright May sun and across a calm and glistening sea. Twice, just after midmorning, our carrier planes bombed U-boat targets off the right flank of the convoy. At 11:30, our destroyers made contact with several submarines dead ahead of the convoy, and we made an emergency turn to starboard and opened fire to port.

The afternoon was quiet, except for occasional depth charge action. Then, just before sundown, one of the carrier planes came in from patrol with empty bomb racks and circled the Commodore's ship and blinked the story of still another successful attack. The Commodore shared the news with the rest of the convoy by running up the flag hoist *GL1=TEZ, "One more enemy submarine destroyed."*

The familiar *WF* went up again at twilight, bright red, blue, and white against a dusky sea, warning us that our foes were at hand again for night action. But if they had made plans to attack, they failed to carry them out. The night passed quietly.

Early the next morning, shortly after sunrise, a huge four-engine Sunderland bomber came winging out from England, circled us twice, and almost immediately found work to be done. She laid her bombs into a submarine that was lying in wait off the starboard bow of the convoy, and again the bright flags *GL1=ETZ* went up on the Commodore's ship. And near noon time, after more action off the starboard flank, the flags read *GL2=ETZ.*

That completed it for our carrier. As abruptly as she had entered the convoy on Sunday with her "Greetings," she now swung out of line, gave us a farewell "Cheerio" on the signal lamp, and turned up her speed to go foaming off toward the south. With her, of course, went her three destroyers.

We watched her out of sight, hoping she would return, but she held straight to her course and disappeared below the horizon, bound for some new assignment. Her task with us, obviously, had been to help us get past the French coast, and now that we were about equidistant between Brest and Ireland—and within protective range of land-based British Sunderlands—that task had been completed. We had sailed directly across the front yard of the submarine pens, passing within 400 miles of the beach, and had fought the wolf pack for five days and nights without losing a ship.

When the sun went down that Thursday evening, there were no submarine warning flags flying from the Commodore's halyards. It was the first time since Sunday that they had been missing at twilight.

Two days later, we rounded Malin Head and Bloody Forelands, swung through the North Channel, and glided into the calm, protective waters of the Irish Sea.

One week later at a convoy conference in Milford Haven, the Royal Navy gave us their figures on our crossing.

"There were twenty-five submarines in the pack," they told us, "and we have reason to believe twelve of them were sunk. All convoy ships arrived safely."

Twelve submarines sunk? I have never believed that figure. Six or eight, possibly, but not twelve.

But without our friends on the escort carrier, and without their clumsy-looking old Swordfish biplanes, the score almost certainly would have been reversed.

CHAPTER SEVEN

STORMY NORTH

FAR UP ON THE NORTHERN RIM OF THE ATLANTIC, there are times when the night holds both beauty and terror in its hands. Those are the nights of chilling blackness, when the giant icebergs flex their glacial muscles, creep down from their Arctic lairs, and lie in wait across the paths of the big ships. Those are the nights when brave sailormen, unafraid of war, stand shivering with fear and try to pretend their trembling is caused by the cold.

The iceberg is a terrible menace, almost unkown today to the ships that follow the normal routes of peacetime commerce between New York and London. But the routes of wartime crossings follow a different course, and many times they intrude upon the iceberg's domain. They lie far to the north, in the bleak waters off Greenland. There the icebergs prowl, and there the convoy ships must run blacked-out at night, like a herd of blind brutes lost in a world of other brutes both blind and deaf.

And the nights are bitterly cold, as cold as the fingers of death.

It was a night late in spring, when the war still had many months to go, that *Gulfwing* and I first met the icebergs. Although it was late spring, the weather over our part of the North Atlantic held a wet and biting chill as punishing and depressing as a midwinter drizzle.

Right from the start, it had been a cheerless convoy. At our departure conference in Wales, at Milford Haven's old South Hook Fort, there had been only a handful of us ready to sail. And three German bombers had attacked us there before we had even raised anchor. Other ships had joined us off Liverpool and off Black Head on the coast of Scotland. Finally, with about fifty ships in all, we had passed out of the North Channel one sundown and had swung our sterns to the shores of Ireland and had sailed off into a cloudy twilight.

I remember standing on the bridge with Ivar, who had the mate's watch, and looking back to where the shadows of purple dusk were coloring the waves, and hearing Ivar say:

"The North Atlantic can be the most beautiful thing God ever made when she wants to be—like now."

"But," he added after a bit, "she can also be the meanest, most treacherous old bitch on the face of the earth when she's mad about anything."

I think she must have been very angry about something that time, for she gave us screaming winds and giant waves and snow and sleet and rain, day after day, night after night, as we moved ever westward.

After nine days, we entered the cold, wet storm belt between Cape Farewell and Newfoundland, and as the hours of evening approached, the rain came to a halt and the gray clouds overhead settled so low that they seemed to be stroking the crow's nest.

We could barely see the Commodore ship out ahead; it loomed like a vague blot in the darkening murk. But we watched it intently, knowing that it was time now to be given our night orders before visibility vanished altogether.

And then they came, the signal flags going aloft on high halyards. There were three flag hoists from the Commodore, one following quickly upon the other:

> *Enemy submarines are at hand.*
> *Expect submarine attack after dark.*
> *Keep full crews at all guns all night.*

Moments later the darkness closed down, and one by one the ships disappeared. They were somewhere close at hand in the wet, black night, but there was no way of telling just where.

By morning it was almost as bad, for we had entered a world of fog so thick and sodden that it was impossible to see the length of the deck. The fog held on, hour after hour all day, until just before evening when it lifted for only a few moments, just long enough for another flag hoist from the Commodore's ship:

> *Entering ice field tonight. Blow signal "U"*
> *upon sighting icebergs.*

Ivar swore under his breath and I could see him shudder.

"They're close," he said. "The icebergs are close."

"How do you know?"

"I've been feeling them for an hour. Feel them in the wind."

He was right. The temperature had been going down and down, and the touch of the wind had been getting more and more frigid. I looked at the thermometer on the bridge. It had dropped below freezing. The wind now was like the breath of a giant arctic refrigerator.

"Better the submarines," Ivar said. "Better any time, the submarines. Better anything on or under the goddam sea than icebergs at night in the fog." He shivered again.

He had reason to. We were sailing blind at ten knots. An iceberg approaching us would be moving on a three-knot current. A collision would rip us open like a sheet of tin and send *Gulfwing* down in less than a minute. And in this water, a man could stay alive—what was it they had said at Little Creek?—about thirty seconds?

It was one-thirty in the morning when we sighted our first one. There had been a faint, fog-dulled warning from a ship up ahead—a muffled blast on her whistle, two shorts and one long—the code letter *U*.

Then there was silence, except for the splashing of the waves along *Gulfwing's* hull and the soft, wet drip of the fog. There was silence and there was a tense period of waiting that seemed to last forever, waiting and straining our eyes to see into the black fog.

Then we heard a sound both strange and frightening like the sound of surf as it breaks on the shore, but we were many miles from land.

There at last it came, with waves rolling in against its bulk, a monstrous, pale white blotch that loomed suddenly in the fog about fifty yards off our starboard bow, a giant iceberg towering mast high, muttering and straining as though to reach out and crush us.

We roared the warning on *Gulfwing's* horn, and an echoing roar bounced back from the monster's icy sides. Then suddenly we were past and the white beast slid astern of us across our wake and vanished in the fog.

All through the hours until dawn, the huge icebergs came and went. Twice in the night, we heard the tortured sound of collision, of metal against ice, of a ship's whistle screaming in distress. But there was no turning back, for a convoy in darkness must stay on course no matter what may happen. Finally after many hours, the blackness thinned and the gray of dawn filtered across the waves, and we were able at last to see where we were going and what might be waiting ahead to threaten us.

By sunrise, the danger was gone. From time to time, icebergs still appeared and made their lumbering way toward our course, heading south to their melting grounds. But in daylight, it was easy to sideslip them.

As dawn broke full, they were beautiful in the glow of sunlight, light green, aquamarine, turquoise, and pure white, shaped in many weird designs of caves and peaks and bridges and pinnacles and minarets. All day long we watched them in wonder.

Finally, about four o'clock that afternoon, the last one came and went, a baby thing that looked like a floating, white toy, and seemed almost panicky as though it had lost its way and knew it could never catch up with its bigger brothers.

The mate had long since stopped trembling, but he was not amused. He spat at the little iceberg as it slipped along our flank and glided astern.

"Bastard!" he said. "Killing bastards, the whole lot of them!"

It was the kindest thing he could have said; it would have been easy to be more expressive.

But a brilliant sort of beauty lies out there too, on the North Atlantic in wartime.

It can come unexpectedly, as it came to us one memorable afternoon, in a dazzling pattern of rainbows that almost reached the indescribable. That was the day when we had passed through a thunder-black hurricane, when the waves had raged so high that we could not see over their tops, and when the tempest had torn our life rafts from their metal beds and hurled them, twisted and broken, into the sea. But the storm passed quickly, and the waves soon lowered from heaving mountains to white-crested hills and knolls.

Suddenly, the sun broke through, sending its warm, golden touch racing across the sea. As it did, it lit up a world of exciting magic and beauty, for it gave to each of the thousands of tossing whitecaps a tiny rainbow of its own. We sailed, dumfounded, in a world of rainbows, tens of thousands of them, so close to the waters that they seemed to be tossing on the wavetops. Rainbows as far as the eye could see, so small and perfect that you felt you could reach out and pick them like flowers and hang them around your neck. Every man aboard ship stood and stared in speechless wonder, held silent by the sheer phenomenal beauty of the sight. After a while the tiny rainbows seemed to drift lazily upward from their sea-borne homes and gradually merge in the sky until they became a single great rainbow that arched high in the heavens, reaching from horizon to horizon before it faded slowly from sight.

Yes, there can be beauty in war, out upon the North Atlantic; in the rising sun that seems not to rise at all but to explode from the east in racing waves of red and gold; in the stars on a quiet night, when they hang low to the gun turrets and the mast tops; and in the great ball of the full moon as it bathes the sea in orange and silver, making black silhouettes of the lightless ships in convoy.

Perhaps there is a kind of beauty on the North Sea, too, and in the Arctic Ocean. But in all our wartime sailing on those brutal waters, we rarely met anything that was not ugly and depressing. We sailed forever, it seemed, in a world where storms were born, where gray and menacing waves would turn into black, raging fury almost in a matter of minutes, where gales shrieked down without warning as though they had been lying in wait for the chance to tear a ship apart.

We learned that it is sometimes impossible to fight a conventional sea battle in the North, for the freezing spray can form thick blocks of ice upon a gun's breech block and firing mechanism. By the time you break the ice from the gun the freezing spray is building ice cakes upon your hands and feet. We learned that there are days at a time when you must live your hours on deck under the protection of a hideous arctic face mask, or your flesh will be cut to ribbons.

We lost a chance to sink a submarine one day in an arctic storm, and the submarine lost her chance, perhaps, to sink us. We were traveling alone, moving down toward Reykjavik at the time, in a gale of sleet and freezing rain that was building a coat of ice upon every exposed inch of the ship. The submarine apparently had run out of torpedoes and was heading for home, perhaps to a pen somewhere on the coast of occupied Norway.

In any event, she appeared on the surface about 2,000 yards off our port bow, already within gun range and bearing on a course that would bring her to within 1,000 yards of us before she passed. She must have been as surprised as we were, for it was several moments before her gunners poured from a hatch and rushed to their deck gun just forward of the conning tower.

Meanwhile, we were helpless. Our guns were iced into position as solidly as though they had been welded, and not one could be moved to train on the target. We thought of using a steam line, but there was no time for that. The submarine was just as badly off; we could see the crew hammering and chopping and doing their best to bring their gun to bear. We considered ramming the U-boat, but it would have been impossible to bring our ship around in the narrowing arc and hold her steady against the pounding of the storm.

We gave up and stood there, and so did the submariners. Our courses converged to their closest point and then we sailed on past, each looking back in frustration as the gap between us widened and we began to pull away in opposite directions. Nobody could do anything about it. Nobody on either side had enough spirit left even to wave or shout insults in passing. In a matter of minutes, we had vanished from each other's sight.

It had been a silent, bloodless engagement; and the Arctic, as usual, was the winner.

CHAPTER EIGHT

AROUND THE ISLES

M ANY OF US WHO FOUGHT THE ATLANTIC WAR IN the convoys have returned, on occasion, since then to the coastal waters of Ireland and the British Isles. But there is never the same magical beauty in making a landfall now as there was in 1942 and 1943.

It could be argued that this is because a landfall in those days of war meant nearing the end of one more death-risk crossing. It meant a respite from ocean perils, a few days in which to relax and enjoy being alive before starting out once more across the broad and heaving sea.

But this cannot be altogether true. The waters around the British Isles at times were less safe in those years than the waters of the mid-Atlantic, for in the open ocean there were only the submarines and the storms and icebergs and collisions to contend with; but around the Isles there were submarines, aircraft, floating mines, frogmen and, in the English Channel, the torpedo-bearing E-boats and even an occasional German surface raider.

Still, it was always good to get over there. Perhaps that was because our ships often went into ports and channels that are rarely visited by travelers in peacetime, places that were strange to us all and that seemed to hold a special, personal, welcoming warmth when we entered.

82

If I live to see Ireland a thousand times, it will never appear more lovely than on that spring evening in 1943 when first we glimpsed Broadhaven and the mountains of Mayo, their shapes looming vague in a blue dusk, many miles off the starboard bow. We had been at sea for fifteen days, and now, suddenly, we were in sight of land again. What's more, it was a land soft and beautiful, and it seemed to reach out to us as though to draw us to an embrace.

We sailed northeast along the coast, tracing our course line on a chart with names that sounded as if they came from an old Irish ballad—Killala Bay, Donegal Bay, Ballyshannon, Rathlin O'Birne.

Twilight lingered with us as we moved close in toward shore, and we cut our speed low for the night hours. With the coming of sunrise, we began a journey of scenic wonder, past great rolling hills that spread their green slopes down to where the surf beat high and white against the seaweed rocks, past dark caves that gaped at the waves, past misty valleys, and always the green and green and green.

There were farmlands, neatly patterned, and there were seemingly endless wild acres of grass and stubby trees, and there were narrow dirt roads that wound down from the hilltops, slanting toward the sea, down past thatched-roof cottages and gaunt stone castles and old ruins of chapels and towers. It was a land of such strange beauty and quiet peace that it seemed almost a sacrilege to be approaching it on a mission of war.

By six o'clock that evening, we had rounded Ireland's northernmost tip, between Inishtrahull and Malin Head. We had passed through the North Channel into the Irish

Sea and were dropping anchor at last in Belfast Lough.

Perhaps it would have been pleasant to stay there a while. There were dozens of Irish townsfolk on the shore, waving a friendly welcome to us, beckoning us to come in. There were golfers on neatly trimmed fairways, and there were restful looking lawns and gardens, as restful looking, that is, as was possible against a background of barrage balloons and antiaircraft batteries, and sunken ships in the harbor.

But when a Royal Navy launch brought our orders out from the beach, we were told to be on our way again, to take our lethal petroleum cargo farther south. We sailed at ten o'clock that night, with the sun still shining, and by midnight we were moving quietly down the Irish Sea, with a bright moon bathing the waters all around us.

The sea next day was as smooth as a garden pool, and the sun shone brightly all day long. The water was a soft and beautiful green. We moved on down past the Isle of Man and Holyhead and northern Wales, changing course slightly near Bishop and Clerk's Lighthouse. Then we turned into St. George's Channel, past the rugged Welsh coastline and the jutting islands of Grassholm and Skokholm, and finally on into Bristol Channel, to tie up at last in the bomb-ravaged port of Swansea.

It had been a memorable introduction to the softer waters of Ireland and the British Isles, from Broadhaven to Worms Head.

For wild and startling beauty, though, the seas and shores farther to the north—the Hebrides Islands and off the lonely Scottish moors—had more to offer.

We first cruised those waters on a February voyage, breaking from convoy near Malin Head and the Irish caves with orders to proceed unescorted to Loch Ewe, on

Scotland's northernmost shore. And so, as the ships that had crossed the Atlantic with us turned southeast toward the Irish Sea, we moved off alone, through snow and fog, heading on a course due north.

The next day's rising sun, with its warmth, seemed almost to turn February into late spring, and it transformed the world around us into a carnival of colors. We were in the Little Minch, that narrow stretch of turbulent sea between the Island of Skye and the Outer Hebrides. For mile after mile and hour after hour, we cruised north past tall, rocky cliffs that reflected every imaginable shade of color in the sun's rays. The cliff walls were honeycombed with great, black caves, some down low at the very edge of the sea and some up high, some dripping with sea weed and some gleaming white with gulls. Bright green waves hurled themselves at the rocks with thundering bursts of spray and flying foam. Watching it all, it seemed you could almost hear the strains and chords of *Fingal's Cave* being played by a great symphony of invisible horns, trumpets, and kettle drums.

There were so many cliffs and tall rocks and craggy islands that, as we stood on the ship's bridge, we began to wonder if an echo might not live forever in such a place, might spring to life and never die. To find out, we decided to fire a shell from our 5-inch gun. The roar of the shot resounded incessantly, like a deafening artillery barrage, and it sent tremendous flocks of sea gulls screaming into the sky. Back and forth the booming sound bounced, up and down, across and sideways. For all I know, it may be echoing there still and may go on to the end of time. That first shot awed us so completely that we never tried a second one.

After a while, as our wake extended ever northward,

the tall cliffs faded away behind us, and the coastline off to starboard changed, slowly but perceptibly, until finally it became the bleak and windswept shore of the northwest highlands.

Then we were passing long stretches of rocks made gray and hoary by the storms of the ages. Scores of ponds and little lakes and dark, deep, large lochs rimmed the seaward edge of the land. The valleys were treeless and wild, dotted here and there with sod-roof cottages and walls of peat. From time to time on the high peaks, we could see fields of snow appearing through rifts in the misty clouds, a hard snow broken in a thousand places by ragged formations of rock. On the lower, rugged hills, the winds of the centuries had swept away every bit of tree growth or tall grass. And at one point we sailed close in-shore past the ruins of an ancient village, complete with crumbling chapel, and with not a living person in sight for miles along the coast.

It was in truth a land that seemed waiting for the wild skirl of bagpipes, or for the chanting of Macbeth's witches, a country offering no apology for its bleakness, its desolate moors, its deep and frothing bays, its angry rivers tumbling toward the sea in white torrents. Rather than an apology, it seemed to offer a take-it-or-leave-it welcome. And we found ourselves drawn to it with a strong, fierce liking.

Then far to the north, as we were rounding the isles, we came at last abeam of Cape Wrath, on Scotland's northwestern tip. And there we went hard right, a full ninety-degree turn, to sail due eastward into one of the most perilous, unmanageable raceways of navigable water known to deep-sea sailormen.

This was Pentland Firth, a narrow, rock-strewn, tidal channel that must have been especially created for the specific purpose of wrecking deep-water ships.

We entered Pentland Firth at Dunnet Head, cloaked in a heavy fog, groping our way along at no more than seven knots, knowing that any sort of vessel might loom up unexpectedly off our bow, anything from an Orkney Islands fishing trawler to a Royal Navy battleship out of nearby Scapa Flow. We knew, too, that there was barely maneuverable room for two ships to pass in opposite directions, especially in the thick, concealing mist.

Scarcely had we entered the channel before our seven-knot speed was abruptly boosted to an astonishing fifteen, for we were caught suddenly in the eastbound tidal rip and were being shot ahead like a canoe in a cataract, more or less out of control. This probably would have been an exhilarating experience in safe waters and under clear sunlight, but not in surroundings of rocks and fog and assorted floating mines that had been dropped by German planes during a raid the night before.

Since there was nothing I could do to help control the ship, I spent my time in the bow with an Enfield rifle, target-shooting at the mines that were bouncing jauntily along beside us. The sport seemed to appeal to my gunners, and they joined in with their 20-millimeter weapons. They scored better than I did.

One of the strangest experiences of that whole tidal sluice-ride came when we overtook a sloop just as it became caught in a tricky swing of the current and found itself pointing back in the direction from which it had come. If that had happened to us, I'm sure we would have frightened any witnesses into heading for the nearest harbor and the nearest pub. After all, ocean-going vessels are not supposed to go charging around backward.

Inevitably there had to be an end, even to Pentland Firth. For us it came as we passed southeast of Scapa Flow and emerged from the thick fog into pale sunlight. We had reached Duncansby Head, the pivot point for a ninety-degree turn south into the North Sea. Ahead of us, far down at the mouth of a watery funnel, lay the English Channel.

At the height of the war, that voyage down the Channel was always one of the most dreaded assignments an Armed Guard officer could find in his sailing orders. It included just about everything he had been trained to guard against.

Overhead by day there were Dornier and Heinkel bombers from the German bases in Norway. For a time, before the channel narrowed, there were submarines, and always there was the danger of surface raiders from the German coast.

At night, you usually ran blacked-out in a heavy fog, and you knew that other ships were running blacked-out too, perhaps bearing down toward a head-on collision. You were cramped for maneuvering space, for at times you were in the middle of the thickest, most deadly mine fields in the world and trying to keep in a swept channel only 600 feet wide. You dared not show a light or make an unnecessary sound because of the German E-boats.

The E-boats, German cousins of our PT-boats, had such a shallow draft and such high speed that they could ignore the threat of mines and dash along above them, barely skimming the surface of the sea, almost like hydroplanes. They enjoyed doing this. They enjoyed cruising across the Channel by night and lurking off the British coast with their bows pointed toward home, hidden in the darkness and the fog, waiting patiently until their detectors told them that a ship was drawing near. Then, as the ship drew even, they would burst out of hiding with a roar of mighty engines and would race back toward home, unleashing their torpedoes as they thundered by. There wasn't much that could be done against them. The best thing to do was just to pray.

In our case, the prayers worked. We handled the Channel run many times, carrying everything from gasoline to bombs. Only once did we get hit, and then it was by a dud torpedo that crashed against our hull and bounded away in a clumsy, backward somersault.

The collective sigh, as we watched it flounder astern, was almost enough to blow away the fog.

That was one of the nights when we retired to the skipper's cabin and broke open a bottle of Scotch.

CHAPTER NINE

TO THE STRAIT AND BEYOND

I N THE FALL OF 1943, WE WERE TAKEN OFF THE British convoy circuit for several weeks and were sent to the Mediterranean—and beyond.

At the time, I had just been given a new ship and a new crew, but I scarcely expected a new sailing route, for the stockpiling in England was well under way by then. We were carrying, along with tanks and jeeps and petroleum, about 7,500 tons of high explosive shells, and it seemed logical to assume that eventually we would be unloading that cargo somewhere on a British pier. That was our feeling as we left New York, in company with thirty-one other convoy ships, five destroyers, and a small galaxy of blimps.

But then came a change of orders. Instead of heading up toward Cape Farewell, we turned south toward Hampton Roads, where we picked up forty more cargo ships, five more destroyers, five destroyer escorts, and an escort aircraft carrier, the U.S.S. *Block Island.*

Out of respect for our cargo, which could have exploded into a seagoing Mt. Pelée, the Convoy Commodore tucked our ship as far back at the tail end of things as he could place us. There we soon learned how a leper must feel. All other ships stayed as far removed from us as possible, and every time we edged up to be sociable we were greeted with the quick flashing of blinker signals urging us to: "Stay away—stay away!" After a while, whenever another ship would inadvertently creep toward us, we would flash our warning first: "Unclean—unclean." We felt better about it, for getting in the first word.

When we were about five hours out of Norfolk, our escorts began dropping depth charges, but since we could see no sign of any submarines, we decided this might be just a planned exercise to keep us on our toes. In any event, they stopped their action just before twilight as the darkening sky turned to the color of mustard, the sea took on a shade of pea green, and the barometer suddenly went into a steady and ominous decline.

What was happening was clear to us all. A tropical hurricane was heading our way.

The storm struck at midnight. It howled in with a rush of giant waves that crashed over our bow. Great torrents of sea water foamed across the foredeck. The ship quivered and shook and groaned, first with her nose buried in the waves and her propellor racing in the air, then with her stern full-under and her bow rearing up like the head of a terrified mare. In the wheelhouse, we gripped the hand rails as we lurched from side to side and wondered whether we would explode by crashing down on some other ship or by having them crash down upon us.

The lightning was incessant, ripping at the sky like savage, white-hot knives. At the height of the storm, around three o'clock in the morning, a Thor-like bolt streaked down from the heavens and shattered the mast of Christmas tree signal lights atop our bridge.

That, apparently, was the climax. The hurricane

roared away then, heading into the northeast, and long before first light the storm had died away to a sulk.

Two days later, as we were idling along in the sunlight off the white sands of Bermuda, we finally got the orders that gave us a destination. We were loafing on deck at the time, enjoying the antics of a spouting whale, two large yellow sea turtles, and a school of flying fish, when word came out from the beach ordering us to keep moving east, that there would be further instructions for us when we reached Egypt.

It was a relaxing voyage across. There were a few submarine alarms and occasional sporadic action, but nothing serious. For the most part, it was a pleasure cruise, calm and warm and peaceful by day, and with a million stars by night blinking above the black gun barrels and reflecting on the gentle waves. For ten restful days, the weather was soft and the breeze was as light as a lover's whisper and the ocean was mile upon mile of long, soothing swells. By day, I wore nothing but shorts, loafers, and a cap. By night, I slept on the bridge with the Milky Way for a blanket.

We passed far to the south of the Azores, and then even farther south to the passage between the Canary Islands and the Madeiras; then at last we turned north to follow the coast of Morocco up past Casablanca and on toward Tangier and the Strait of Gibraltar.

We were about off Rabat when the balmy weather left us. When it went, it departed with a rush. The sun that had stayed with us for so long vanished abruptly just before twilight, the sea turned black and choppy, and great, thick clouds came boiling out from inland Africa, whipping us with hot winds and dust. Then, suddenly, a monstrous wall of blinding rain came roaring out across the sea and wrapped the whole convoy in drenching blackness.

The deluge was so heavy that it flattened the ocean outright before the waves recovered their strength, reared up, and began to climb. Livid flashes of bright, red lightning rode with the storm and crackled around the gun barrels and the mast tops.

The rain was still pouring down like a waterfall, and the sky was as black as tar, when at eleven o'clock that night we came within inches of destruction.

It happened when we suddenly heard the roaring blast of a ship's whistle, close to our starboard beam. One sickening look from the bridge told the story: a gasoline tanker in the next column had lost steering control and was bearing down upon us, her bow looming in the storm and foaming straight toward our starboard quarter.

We went hard right and full ahead. The ship responded barely in time, heeling over sharply, and moments later thousands of tons of gasoline and high explosives plunged past each other, beam to beam, with scarcely enough room for a man's hand between their hull plates.

We worked desperately to swing back, for by then we were running straight through the blacked-out convoy at right angles to its course. We got back on bearing just in time to avoid another munitions ship as it careened across our bow—and just in time to hear another warning blast from a second gasoline tanker.

It was unbelievable that two tankers in one convoy should go out of control without warning and within minutes of each other. Yet it was happening before our eyes. Then, almost simultaneously, both ships switched on

their twin red "No Control" lights, and we held our
breath as we stared through the rain and saw that they
were running helplessly on a collision course.

They struck on an angle, beam to beam, and their
steel plates screeched in the night. For one instant, time
seemed suspended as we waited for the explosion and the
burst of flame. But by some freak of fate, nothing had
sparked. And within minutes, both ships had swung away
and were falling back out of convoy, their red lights
glowing like hot coals.

Death could scarcely have come closer and still missed.

One night later, death did visit our convoy, but not
aboard any ship of ours. It happened, instead, to an intruder.

We were approaching Cape Spartel at the time, making ready to change convoy formation and turn in toward
Gibraltar. It was twilight, and we had been sailing at slow
speed all day in order to kill off the sunlight hours and
enter the Mediterranean after dark, concealed from the
eyes of the enemy.

Just at dusk, a big fishing trawler came over the west-
ern horizon, and as she approached us she turned on her
running lights. We put the glasses on her, and saw that
she was Portuguese. We shrugged. She had a right to
show her lights, for technically she was a neutral vessel.

But as full darkness came down and we made a
change of course, she deliberately dropped back and fell
about one mile astern of us and came trailing along with
her lights burning brightly.

A destroyer on our beam flashed her a warning to stay
away or darken her lights. She ignored the order.

We altered course again; and so did she. We warned

her again, and once more altered course; she moved right along in our wake, shifting whenever we did, altering speed whenever we did. By intent or not, she was using her bright mast lights in a way that could keep a watching enemy aware of the exact course and speed of the big, blacked-out convoy.

There was only one thing to do, and our destroyer did it. A final warning was sent and ignored. That was the signal for the end.

A single, booming shot roared out from the destroyer's 5-inch gun. Suddenly, where the fishing boat had been, there was nothing—no boat, no lights, and no more betrayal.

We changed convoy formation then, from twelve columns to two, and went through the strait quietly and under a blanket of heavy darkness.

Next dawn, we crawled at slow speed off the coast of Spain, hidden from shore by a curtain of gray rain and barely making headway while we waited for a convoy of thirty ships from Britain to join our columns.

The skipper stood with me on the bridge as we watched the ships take up their new formation. The weather made him feel good.

"Nobody on shore can see us in this rain," he gloated. "Here's one convoy that won't be reported to old Hitler."

He was wrong, of course. We had scarcely assumed formation, twelve columns wide again, before two Spanish fishing boats came chugging along through the dirty weather. They moved up to a position just off the main channel and about one mile ahead of the convoy. There they hove to, and slung their fishing nets overboard.

There was nothing anybody could do about it; certainly a Spaniard has a right to fish in the Mediterranean, war or no war.

But it was obvious that they had put themselves in an ideal location to count all the ships as we steamed on by, to make a leisurely inventory of the deck cargoes, and to check the number of fuel tankers and escort ships.

We heard all about it that night when we turned on our radio and monitored the English language news broadcast from Berlin. It told us a lot that we already knew.

"A huge Allied convoy of more than one hundred merchant ships and twenty escorting warships entered the Mediterranean through the Strait of Gibraltar before dawn today," Berlin said. "Deck cargoes included tanks, trucks, heavy artillery pieces, torpedo boats, and about one hundred railway locomotives. Our aircraft and submarines have been alerted and are preparing a warm welcome, at a time and place of their own choosing. The convoy will be destroyed."

Early next morning, we swung over to the coast of North Africa. The weather cleared, and we moved eastward all that day under ideal cruising conditions. The sea was without a ripple, and the October sun blazed down as though it were midsummer. The men stood watch at their guns in shorts and helmets.

Twice in the afternoon, German reconnaissance planes flew out from France and looked us over from several miles away, well beyond effective firing range. Each time they did, American Airacobra fighter planes appeared as though out of nowhere and sent the big aircraft hurrying back toward home.

All in all, it was a pleasant Mediterranean voyage. For the most part, we stayed close to the African coast as we worked our way slowly eastward, stopping at one port after another, sometimes breaking off ships from convoy and sometimes absorbing others that were bound for ports farther along on our route. We visited the dirty city of Oran, where it squatted in its coastal amphitheater. We beat off a submarine attack at night between Algiers and Bougie, and an attack by Stuka dive bombers the following morning. By day, as we journeyed on toward Tunis, the mountains along the coast seemed to grow higher and higher with each passing mile, and the tall cliffs leered down upon the water. By night, the bright African moon shone across the mountain sides, and sent pools of light rippling out across the sea.

By night, too, there were the hospital ships, sailing along with lights ablaze in a world of blackout and tension. You could see them approaching from far, far away, looking ironically like gay carnival showboats, with their entire outline gleaming brightly, with a broad band of green lights along the rails and a huge, illuminated, red cross shining on the hull plates and reflecting across the water. For three nights they passed us, bound west from Italy, in traffic so steady that at one time five of them went by within a two-hour period after midnight. When we came to the harbor of Bizerte, there were still more of them at hand, unloading their wounded at the docks.

From Bizerte we moved across the Gulf of Tunis, past ancient Carthage, and slipped around Cape Bon under a rising moon. Then came Sicily, and Pantelleria, the one-time Italian stronghold that had surrendered to a lone aircraft. And Lampedusa. And Malta. We were always dropping off ships, occasionally picking up one or two, and always heading eastward, past tremendous island-rocks that had known the Phoenicians and the Roman galleys, where ancient tales had peopled the mist-wreathed peaks with gods and goddesses.

There were incidents along the way, of course. There was the night off Bengasi, when we were running parallel to the coastal highway where Rommel and the British had fought their private war. The moon was overcast and the sea was cloaked in shadows, and a pale, thin light shone down on the desert sands of Libya. That was the night German bombers hit Bengasi and spotted us below as they flew back toward the continent, and returned to us in a diving attack that ripped open the darkness with fiery tracer bullets. And there was another night when they came at us with bombs. And still another night, when they struck at Tobruk while we were in the harbor, blasted a fuel dump with a tremendous eruption of flame, and gunned our decks as they roared back across the sea toward Crete.

But we came through it all unharmed, with our 7,500 tons of high explosives unscratched. We moved on to Port Said and Suez, to the Red Sea, to the offshore stink of Karachi, and finally into the heavy, brassy heat of the Persian Gulf, where the temperatures soared up past 125 degrees and where we kept wet blankets draped over our ammunition to protect it from the sun.

There we turned around and started back. New orders had come crackling in over the radio. They told us to return to Egypt, to unload at Alexandria, and to stay there over Thanksgiving Day. That sounded agreeable. We had much to be thankful for.

CHAPTER TEN

CROSSROADS OF EGYPT

WHEN WE SAILED FROM EGYPT, AFTER A MONTH IN port, we departed from Alexandria with orders to return to New York. We sailed with a ballast cargo of scrap metal made up of battered tanks, helmets, shell casings, bayonets, machine guns, artillery pieces, swords, rifles, and machetes, all scooped up from the hot desert sands of El Alamein.

We sailed also with the memory of a thousand impressions and surprises, for Egypt in 1943 was a crossroads of many armies and navies, of appetites and tempers, of intrigue and vengeance, of hope and despair, and of all manner of human tides, both physical and emotional. Egypt was something you could scarcely believe while you were there, but could never forget after you had left.

It was a relief to be at sea again, and to get away from flies and rats and fleas, from the filth and the crushing heat, from the stench and the diseased water and the spoiled food and the cut-rate crime market that operated at ten piasters (or forty cents) per murder.

But it was a little sad to be leaving the friendly ones, the Egyptians who hated the British and were still cheering for Rommel, but who liked the Americans. They would dog along at our heels on the street, calling out

over and over again: "Good American—say hello, please."
They would ask when Franklin D. Roosevelt was coming
over to rule the world from Cairo.

Egypt was luxury: The magnificent palace of Ras el
Tin on the Alexandria waterfront; the plush apartments
in the European section of the city; the palm-lined boulevards and the ocean drives along the Mediterranean, like
a touch of old Newport or Narragansett Pier, set down by
chance in the Middle East; the parks and estates, bright
with marble and fountains and velvety lawns; the never-
ending parade of Rolls-Royce limousines along the avenues.

And Egypt was poverty: the squalor and filth of the
native quarters, with millions of flies swarming over the
open counters of shrimp and fish and decayed fruit; the
children playing naked in the garbage-filled gutters; the
goats and sheep and cows asleep on hot pavements; the
thousands of dirty men garbed in rags, screaming and
cursing at each other but never letting up in their scratch-
ing; the beggars asleep on the sidewalks and in the streets,
with their faces masked by crawling insects.

Egypt was the street vendor: Vendors carrying their
huge urns of silver and copper, selling drinks of hot licorice
or coffee or cold lemonade; vendors selling drugs, women,
and pornography; selling tickets to peep shows and ob-
scene movies and perverted exhibitions; selling the services
of male prostitutes and of brothels staffed by little girls
not yet in their 'teens; selling bracelets and jewelry and
silks and leather goods and knives.

Egypt was uniforms: The uniforms of officers and men
of many nations, sightseeing along the boulevards, sprawl-
ed unconscious in the back alleys, crowding into the cafes
and restaurants at cocktail time; the uniforms of Sikhs,

Gurkas, and Senegalese; of wild desert tribesmen; of British and Greek and American troops; of Polish and Norwegian and Belgian forces; of the French Foreign Legion; the Egyptian police; the camel cavalry; the Red Cross.

Egypt was the stiff protocol of the Middle East Command by day and the enchantment of old Cairo by night. It was a martini on the terrace of Shepheard's Hotel at dusk while watching the long, white fingers of searchlights groping for enemy planes overhead. It was a camelback ride to the Pyramids and the Sphinx. It was the view from the Mohamed Aly mosque, looking down upon the city of Cairo as it lay bathed in a flaming sunset. It was the Nile, with the motion of ancient barges and curved sails. It was the native bazaar after dark, with its cacophony of strange chants and cries and lights and smells, and occasionally a body in the street with its throat cut.

Egypt was moonlight. It was a train ride from Cairo to Alexandria across the flat Nile delta region, watching the soft, white, lunar glow reflecting upon sand dunes and canals and palm trees and native villages, and upon the white sails of the river boats. It was the moonlight spilling across the harbor at Alexandria, shining upon the oldest lighthouse in the world, and upon British cruisers and Greek destroyers and Egyptian gunboats, and upon tall minarets and antiaircraft guns, and upon the wailing Arab stevedores as they worked all night unloading our ship.

Sometimes there would be an alert, and enemy aircraft would come in from over the sea, silently and swiftly. Then the Arabs would scream, "Bombs!—Bombs!" and scramble from the ship like ants. The brilliant searchlight shafts would stab the sky and, perhaps, catch a plane in a pool of silver, and hold it there while the guns barked and thundered from below. The Arabs had good reason to scream and run, for Alexandria held ugly bomb scars, most of them left over from a night when the Axis planes had deliberately attacked the squalid native quarters and had touched off huge fires and killed more than 500 persons in an attempt to start a city-wide panic.

To remember Egypt as it was in wartime is to remember far more than just the backwash of war itself. There were other things to do there besides fight a war, and ample time for doing them.

We went, more than once, on visits to Alexandria's ancient ruins, down into the deep tombs and the cool, underground halls of people who had lived there more than 3,000 years ago. We dug bits of old pottery from the dirt and the sand, and we paused reflectively at the tomb of Alexander the Great. We admired the cold, stone statues of figures that were said to be those of Antony and Cleopatra, and agreed that perhaps they were. We watched archeologists at work, scientists indifferent to the fact that the world around them was at war. We shared their excitement when they dug into the side of a deep ditch and salvaged ancient lamps and vases and bits of precious jewelry.

We rode by day in the rickety old taxicabs with their squawking French horns, and by night in the horse-drawn gharries with their jingling bells. We regularly joined the cocktail crowd at Pastraudi's restaurant, the gathering place for the Egyptian *Who's Who* of military and naval and diplomatic affairs.

It was at Pastraudi's that we played cards and drank beer with Australian officers, repatriated after two years in the Nazi prison camps. They were angry and bitter, but they were eager to talk. They told of being beaten and whipped, and of being forced to stand motionless in their prison compound for hours at a time, and if they moved, they were shot and killed. They told of other prisoners who had been deliberately starved to death, and of frightened German soldiers cutting off their own right hands upon being ordered to the Russian Front. They told of being paraded through the streets of German towns, and of how the people who lived there tried to storm through the ring of guards and attack them with clubs and knives in revenge for British and American air raids. All of these Australians had been captured in Greece, and for that they blamed the English. They accused the English of evacuating all the Tommies and leaving the Aussies with only a small force of tanks to fight the advancing German army.

Perhaps they were telling the truth. Perhaps not. If we were sometimes skeptical, it was simply because everybody in Egypt seemed to hate the English, and after a time the conversations seemed like a contest to see who could tell the most lurid stories of English perfidy.

Everyone hated the Italians, too, even though Italy had surrendered and now was presumed to be friendly. The troops who had been held in Italian prison camps loudly maintained that there was no atrocity story from any German prison camp that they could not match and top. The Italian prison guards, they declared, were the most arrogant and cruel of the lot, and if it were left up to the ex-prisoners to run the war, they would turn the Allied armies loose in Italy to rape and loot and kill, and to show the Fascists what war was really like.

The bitter rantings against the Italians always got

around to the fact that, with cigarettes selling at one dollar a package, the British and American troops in Egypt had just been put on half rations; the missing half, they pointed out, was being distributed to their new "allies," the Italians. That was always a subject for hot discussion at Pastraudi's bar.

And so, we took away many memories, when at last we sailed from Egypt.

We remembered how the brilliance of sunrise and sunset would splash livid colors across the walls of the whitewashed buildings. We remembered the crisp, chill feel of nightfall, after daylight hours of heat and sweat; the arrival of Roosevelt, Churchill, and Chiang Kai-shek for their Cairo Conference; the Thanksgiving Day football game between two American Army teams, the remarks of the bewildered spectators who were seeing the sport for the first time, and the splendid between-the-halves parade of the gold-braided, leopard-skinned, Alexandria Police Bagpipe Band, complete with kilties.

We remembered the little perfume shops in the darkest heart of the Cairo bazaar; the weird City of the Dead on the outskirts of Cairo, where the Moslems had built homes and laid out streets for their departed friends; the magnificent Arabian steeds drawing rickety stevedore wagons along the Alexandrian waterfront; the shopkeepers who would break off their haggling at the sound of the muezzin's call, would kneel and pray to the East, and then would jump up shouting: "One minute for business, one minute for God! Make it eighty piasters!"

There was so much to remember as we sailed away. There was the dockside scene of the British soldiers mercilessly clubbing an Arab stevedore who had dropped a case of ammunition overside while helping to unload a ship; of the little, ragged boy who screamed defiance and shook his finger in the face of a British sergeant, punched the soldier in the stomach, but did not run away; of the night when thousands of Arabs rioted against the French and rushed screaming down the street, brandishing clubs and knives, and in all the confusion carefully avoided laying a finger on any American.

Then there were the perfumed women of Cairo, parading the streets at sundown with their leashed baboons; the stillness of Alexandria just before dawn, when the only sound to break the hush would be the tinkling bells of the gharries; the search for Egyptian newspapers aboard all Allied ships bound for England, to make certain that the story of the Cairo Conference and the hate-British incidents would not get out to the world too soon; the bite of the Egyptian fly, bringing chills and high fever and twenty-four hours of dysentery; the constant dredging operations in the harbor at Alexandria, trying to salvage part of the thousands of tons of food, medicine, weapons, and munitions that were dumped there when Rommel had stood at El Alamein and when Mussolini was about to enter the city on a white stallion.

All this we remembered, when at last it came time to sail, and when we cast off our lines and moved slowly out across the harbor, looking back from the bridge on the scene of experiences that seemed more than half unreal.

It had been a fantasy, and yet it had been realism. It had been a caricature of wartime living that could have no duplication anywhere else in the world.

We had enjoyed it, but we were glad to leave. It was time now to return to the duels with the aircraft and the

submarines, to the heaving Atlantic waves that were waiting for us out beyond the Mediterranean.

Others could go on fighting the war at Pastraudi's and
at Shepheard's Hotel. Our orders were to get back into it
with the rest of the convoy gunners.

CHAPTER ELEVEN

PETS AFLOAT

WHEN WE SAILED FROM EGYPT, WE TOOK A FRIENDLY, brown-haired female along with us, and she became so popular that we kept her aboard after that, wherever we went. Her name was Trixie.

She was an underfed mongrel puppy, surviving on hopes and gutter scraps, when two of the gunners found her and adopted her and brought her to the ship on our last night in Alexandria. After that, until the time I left the ship many months later, I never knew Trixie to set paw on dry land again, and for all I know she may have spent all the rest of her life at sea. That would have pleased her; she was a born sailor.

Trixie was the last of a unique line of pets that accompanied us on voyages over a long period of time. She was, in one way at least, the best of the lot; she was the only one that stayed.

We began our parade of animals with a marmoset from Brazil and a parrot from Panama, the property respectively of two petty officers aboard *Gulfwing*. Nobody ever liked the marmoset. He was bad tempered and, also, quite obviously, homesick. He didn't stay with us for very long. He sat on the stern rail gazing off toward the horizon all one cloudy afternoon as we moved slowly up the

East Coast toward New York. Then, as evening approached, he turned around for a last, contemptuous look at the bridge and coolly jumped overboard. Somehow he fought free of the propellor wash, and started dog-paddling back in the direction of South America. He didn't get very far; he was such a poor swimmer, he'd have drowned in a bathtub.

The parrot lasted longer and in time became a good talker, but since his instructors were merchant seamen and Navy gunners, his vocabulary was somewhat parochial. He used most of it to provoke a bitter feud with the ship's cook, a surly Chinese with whom he developed an acute case of mutual hatred. The feud never reached its full peak, though, until one of the sailors, a China coast veteran, taught the parrot to swear in Cantonese. Then the shrieks that came from the galley were enough to chill the blood.

One afternoon a gunner discovered that the parrot's cage was empty and its door wide open. A thorough search of the ship failed to turn up the missing bird.

The cook, of course, was a natural suspect. Accordingly, he was collared at his galley stove and grilled by five or six gunners, but he went into his "No speakee" act of pretending not to understand English. At that, a seaman finally brought in the empty bird cage and pointed at it and hollered: "Where go? Where go?"

"Ohhh," said the cook. He grinned and nodded. "You say where go blird?—He fly!" And he turned back to his pots and gravies with an obvious air of dismissal.

The crew gave up and left the galley.

That night at dinner, the cook personally carried in a meat pie and placed it on the table and then departed without a word. Nobody had the courage to taste it, which apparently neither surprised nor offended the contented chef.

Long before Trixie came aboard, we had another dog that joined the Navy. She made four crossings with us before getting permanent shore leave for circumstances beyond her control—defiance of British Admiralty laws.

Her name was Eloise, applied to her in honor of the girl friend of a fat, bearded gunner's mate from Tennessee.

Eloise was barely the size of a man's hand when one of the crew picked her up at a New York pet shop on the eve of a departure for England. She was a furry, little Sheltie, mostly white with a few blotches of black, and she was so unsteady on her legs that she had a hard time at first keeping her balance in a moderate sea. When the ship ran into waves of any size, Eloise would curl up like a ball of yarn and go rolling back and forth across the deck until some passing gunner picked her up and put her inside his shirt.

Nevertheless, she gained strength and weight quickly. She got fed every time there was a change of watch and at various times between meals. One day she ate seven pork chops between noon and sundown.

In spite of her diet, she stayed healthy and playful. She enjoyed being brought up to the signal bridge, where she was allowed to roll around in the sun. She liked to sit there and growl at the seagulls, but she would run for cover whenever one of them swooped down too close. By general consent, she became the property of every man in the gun crew and not of any individual. That was a convenient arrangement enabling anyone who went broke in a game of blackjack or poker to sell Eloise to anybody else at the table. From week to week, she brought prices ranging from fifty cents to ten dollars, and the good thing about her was that she could be resold a hundred times and still be as marketable as new.

Eloise went through several submarine and air attacks with us, but she never did get adjusted to the sound of guns and the jarring thump of depth charges. To her, the crack of gunfire was always a signal to race around in mad circles, wetting as she went.

The British authorities at Liverpool voiced strong objections against Eloise the first time she visited their port. They marched aboard with their badges and papers and documents to make their customs and health inspections and, of course, they met Eloise immediately. She bounded up to greet them, no doubt mistaking them for another source of pork chops.

" 'ere now," they said gravely. "None of that now. No dogs in port, chaps. That's the rule. We just can't 'ave it, y'know."

When we promised not to let her go ashore and never to bring her back again, they spared her life. By chance, though, we returned to Liverpool three months later, and Eloise was still a member of the ship's company. Unfortunately, the same officials with the same badges and papers came aboard. They were outraged at finding her there.

"Now then, we warned you chaps," they said. "We've our rules to obey, y'know, same as you. And where would we all be if everybody ran around breaking the Admiralty laws?"

They were all for shooting Eloise on the spot.

Fortunately, we were able to persuade the U.S. Navy

and the War Shipping Administration to intercede for a
stay of execution, but in return we had to give our word
never again to bring Eloise into British waters. There was
nothing to do, therefore, but to put her ashore perma-
nently, which we did when we returned to New York. We
fed her a farewell pork chop and locked her in a crate
and shipped her off to the family of one of the crew members who lived in a southern New England town.

Months later we learned that her new owners loved
Eloise warmly, but were baffled by one of her peculiar
habits. Every time a door slammed or an automobile back-
fired, she would leap up and race around in mad circles,
wetting as she went.

We had no legal troubles whatever with our next two
pets, for they minded their own business and kept to themselves and never violated any rules of the British Admiralty.

They were twin cockroaches, and they lived in the
wheelhouse. For indentification purposes they were
known simply as George and Henry. The names were
unimaginative, but they were settled upon by a quartermaster called Tex; he argued that if he had to go
through life with a trite nickname, so at least should the
cockroaches.

"And do you realize they've crossed with us three
times?" Tex said to me one day. "I think they're just a
pair of glory-chasers, hanging around for campaign ribbons."

George lived on the wheelhouse shelf where we made
our coffee. His diet included sugar, evaporated milk, and
coffee grounds, both fresh and used. For a time we worried
a little about whether he was getting enough exercise, so

I had Simon the signalman take him off the shelf and put him out for a run on deck every evening when we stood our twilight submarine watch. George was always back at his post on the shelf in time for breakfast.

We had a serious crisis with him one day, or rather he had a crisis of his own until we rescued him. It happened when he was making his customary exploration trip through the opening of a can of evaporated milk. He had been putting on weight, and now he got stuck at his midriff.

Poor George just hung there with his head out of sight and his hind legs waving in the air, until Tex happened to glance over from the wheel and notice him.

"Hey there, Lieutenant," he said. "Look at old George. You want to take the wheel and I'll help him? That must hurt like hell."

"I'll help him," I said. I hadn't even noticed.

It was quite a job to get George eased out of the can without any fatal injuries. He didn't help matters any by getting panicky and thrashing around. But I worked him free after a while, and he scuttled off to recover behind a fig newton.

After that it seemed to me that he stayed away from can tops and waited for his milk until we spilled a little for him on the shelf.

Henry was a different type entirely. Henry the Navigator, we called him. He lived in the ship's compass.

We never knew how he got in there, nor how he managed to get enough food to stay alive. But he did, and he was healthy.

He would ride there on the compass circle, always facing forward and never getting off course. If we were heading southeast on course 135, Henry would be riding exactly on 135 degrees. If the Convoy Commodore ordered a course change and we swung up to 110 degrees, Henry would wait until we were squarely on our new bearing and then scamper right over from 135 to 110 and take up his new position.

The glass disc that magnified the compass points sometimes made Henry look like a rather unreal monster, and when we stared down at him he would brandish his feelers like swords. We often wondered what we must look like to him, but whatever it was, it never frightened Henry. He would just stand there behind the glass, day and night, rolling with the ship, and occasionally stamping over from 275 degrees to 250 or somesuch, and always staying on course.

Tex claimed that Henry was an old-time mariner. "Look at the way the son of a bitch rides! He's been to sea before, you can tell by his legs."

One time we discussed the advisability of removing the compass cover and handing Henry some bread and jam. We decided it wasn't worth the risk; it might injure the instrument and take us right out of convoy. And Henry wouldn't have liked that any better than we would. Furthermore, he seemed to be thriving on whatever it was he ate and drank.

"Take it from me," said Tex. "When nobody's looking, that little guy sneaks down and has himself a nip of the alcohol in the compass base."

And perhaps he did.

Anyhow, when the sea and the sky and the ship and everything else would be quiet with the blackness of night, it was always reassuring to stand in the wheelhouse and

hear George rustling around on top of the sugar jar, or to
turn on the dim red light above the compass dial and see
Henry glaring up from inside with his feelers aloft and his
knees bending with the roll of the ship.

Among the other forms of wildlife that sailed with us
on the war lanes were uncounted dozens of earthworms.
I believe we carried the only seagoing worm farm that
ever traveled in convoy.

The worms were the crop and property of a gunner
named Fosdick, who must have been one of the most
dedicated fishermen in the Navy. Fosdick reasoned that
no bait was as tempting, delectable, and irresistible to a
hungry fish as a fat, healthy, all-American worm, and
since the worm crop in distant parts of the world might
be skimpy or even nonexistent, the smart thing to do
would be to breed and raise them as he went along.

With this in mind, he reported aboard ship off Staten
Island with two sacks of worms and loam, fresh from the
rich soil of a New Jersey truck farm. By nightfall of his
first day, he had talked the ship's carpenter into building
him a wide but shallow wood-frame box, into which he
dumped his loam and worms and then carefully leveled
off the surface. From there on, he was in business.

Every port we touched, from Iceland to Libya, found
Fosdick trying to sell bait worms to other fishermen in the
crew, and in between ports he carried on a persistent sales
campaign.

He even advertised his worms in the crew's mess, on
the National Maritime Union's bulletin board: "Nep-
tunian Nightcrawlers—10 cents each, $1 a dozen. See
Fosdick, Navy Gun Crew."

He encouraged audience participation in his daily

chore of worm-feeding, when he would scatter sugar on
the surface of his worm bed and sprinkle a little milk on
the loam or toss in a handful of crushed corn flakes. Usually he kept his boxed pets under cover near the ship's
stack—"Where they can absorb a little warmth," he explained—but sometimes he would move them out into the
open sunlight, or let them enjoy a mild downfall of soft
rain. He always kept two or three plump specimens in a
display bottle, to show off to prospective buyers.

The worms thrived. The only trouble was that they
could not catch fish. In port after port, Fosdick would load
his hooks with healthy-looking nightcrawlers, cast out into
deep water, and wait for the action that never came.
Meanwhile, the other fishermen aboard would bait up
with galley scraps—with old bacon, salt pork, or a strip
of sirloin—cast into the same waters, and pull up codfish,
perch, eels, halibut, or whatever happened to be swimming around.

Fosdick never caught a thing.

"Maybe you haven't flavored them right," a sympa-
thetic gunner told him one day. "Maybe they're too sweet
with sugar or too flat with dry cereal. Why don't you try
some spices?"

Fosdick gave him a cold sneer and told him to get lost.
After the twilight watch that night, we noticed him
spreading a generous layer of mustard over a section of
the worm bed, but still the fish wouldn't bite.

Probably sooner or later the situation would have re-
solved itself, with Fosdick just giving up on the whole
thing. But we didn't have to wait for that; Eloise forced
the issue.

As we lay at anchor in a Scottish loch one day, she

discovered that a box of dirt provides a special and natural sanitation convenience in the life of a young dog. Never having known this before, she was delighted with her find. She used the box over and over again until Fosdick caught her at it and roared down upon her like a tornado, whereupon Eloise scooted off across the deck, leaving a damp trail behind her.

Fosdick hesitated a moment, torn between chasing after her and housecleaning his worm farm. Then, moving in grim silence, he picked the whole thing up, box and all, heaved it overboard and stalked below.

That was the end of his special project. Next day he was fishing off the stern with the other gunners, using a slice of calves liver for bait, and finally catching fish.

Those were the pets that sailed with us before Trixie came aboard at Alexandria, and decided she had found a home.

She was, in all truth, the best of the seagoing lot. She was affectionate. She watched her diet and never gorged on pork chops. She house-broke herself after choosing a permanent corner on the well deck, where as often as not the sea would foam aboard and rush down the scuppers and clean up after her. Best of all, she joined the gun crew.

That was her own idea—the result of her own intelligence and self-training.

Her bed was back aft, in the crew's quarters immediately under the 5-inch gun platform. For a time, she was bewildered by the fact that every once in a while a brassy gong over her head would burst into a loud clanging and all the men in sight would go rushing out and scramble up an eight-foot vertical ladder to the gun deck overhead. General Quarters had her puzzled.

She worked it out for herself, though, without bothering anybody. One morning when the gong clanged out with a submarine alarm, Trixie dashed out on deck ahead of everybody else and went straight up the ladder like a frightened steeplejack.

From then on, she never missed a GQ, and she was always the first at the gun.

I have said that Trixie was the best of the lot of all the seagoing pets. But something still has to be said for one who was partly seagoing and partly airborne, who traveled with us for two weeks, but who never fully relaxed enough to join our company.

A little yellow bird flew aboard our ship one morning off Hampton Roads as we were heading out for another voyage to the Mediterranean.

She was a tiny, fragile thing, smaller than the average canary, and much more timid. She joined us as we were almost out of sight of land, and she seemed exhausted and frightened as she came to a shivering rest on the signal bridge.

We left her alone. We were afraid we might frighten her into flying off again, and she looked in no condition for that.

By sundown that first day, she definitely had made up her mind to stay. She flew up and down the ship, exploring her new surroundings. For her home, she finally chose a sheltered spot in the storage rack on the boat deck, where Karl the steward kept his sacks of potatoes. That made it easy for her to have breakfast in bed, or a midnight snack, although it presented a risk to her waistline.

From then on, all the way across the Atlantic and into the Mediterranean, she was more or less with us. She

would fly off occasionally, making the long flight from one
convoy column to the next, and perching from time to
time on some other ship. She looked pitifully delicate
when she did that, darting above the big waves as though
scared to death but determined not to show it. Wherever
she went, she always returned to us by sundown, sometimes struggling hard against the wind but always getting
back to where she belonged. After a while, she grew so
unafraid of us that she would fly into the ship's passageways, and one time she made it all the way in to the crew's
mess, where the gunners offered her a bowl of shredded
wheat.

She was still with us as we lay off the harbor at Algiers
one late afternoon, while we waited for a convoy section
to come out and form up with us. She had joined us on
the signal bridge just before sundown; suddenly she dart-
ed up from the deck and perched on the rail, and stayed
motionless there for a long time with her head outstretched
toward the African coast.

Then, abruptly, she soared into the air and took off on
a straight, swift course for the shore, and the last we saw
of her she was fading from sight in the direction of the
hills and the desert sand.

All the next day, we kept looking for her to return.
But she never came back.

We hoped she'd be happy in her new African home.
It had been nice knowing her.

CHAPTER TWELVE

DOUR SCOTLAND

WHEN NEXT WE RETURNED TO THE BRITISH ISLES, after the long side trip to the Middle East, it was to sail up the River Clyde and drop anchor in Loch Long.

We had been to Scotland before, but we had never stayed long enough to spend a night ashore and mix with the people. We knew they were supposed to be dour and plain, half-vinegar and half-oatmeal. But that was before we arrived in the lake country and journeyed from there to Glasgow and discovered Sauchiehall Street and the Piccadilly Club.

Loch Long made a beautiful anchorage. The waters were deep and dark, and they were walled in on three sides by crags and cliffs and high, green, rolling hills. Most of the time, as we lay at anchor, it was misty or raining, and the tops of the hills were hidden by the low, moving clouds. The beauty of the place lay in the gray-green of its countryside, in the mysterious blackness of its deep water, and in the way the sun sometimes would shaft its rays through the scudding clouds and turn the moist fields and slopes into vast spreads of sparkling brilliance.

As soon as we had anchored, I took a launch ashore to visit the Navy Liaison Office at Gourock, to turn in my watch schedule and voyage report, and to pick up liberty passes for the crew. The Navy lieutenant at the desk appeared genuinely unhappy over the prospect of twenty or thirty Armed Guard gunners coming ashore with their pockets full of pay.

"Tell your men not to walk alone at night in Greenock," he said morosely.

"They don't know where Greenock is," I said.

"It's the only town around here that's alive," he told me, "so they'll find it after they've been ashore an hour or two."

"Of course."

"But the trouble is," he went on, "a bunch of Greenock teen-agers who aren't old enough to get into the general war have started a private war of their own against lone people in uniform. They roam the streets at night in packs of ten or fifteen. They carry bicycle chains over their shoulders, hidden under their jackets. When they see a man in uniform walking alone, they slip up behind him, sling the chain around his throat, and yank it. They've discovered that this breaks the neck. Last week they killed two Canadians and put two others in the hospital."

"How about Americans?" I asked.

He shrugged. "Not yet."

I sent the liberty passes and the gloomy warnings back to the ship in the care of a petty officer, and then I took the next train to Glasgow, only an hour's ride away.

The Captain and I had rooms at the North British Station Hotel, as guests of an American oil combine. It was a two-man delegation from that outfit that introduced us to the Piccadilly Club.

Glasgow, we had been told in New York, had been beaten to its knees by the long months of war. The shortages were acute, the children were hungry and without milk, whole families had become scavengers. Standing outside the hotel that night, waiting for the oil combine's limousine, we believed all that because just down a side street we could see shawled women prowling barefoot in the rain and poking into garbage cans for whatever food they might find.

We watched them for a few moments, and then we went off to the club, reflecting that if we were lucky, from the way things looked, we might get a dinner of dry toast and Brussels sprouts. We remembered ruefully that it was steak night back aboard ship.

But it was steak night at the club too, steak or sex or silliness, rare or well done. Once you got inside, you pretty much had your choice.

The Piccadilly was exclusive. If you were a stranger, you got in only by having somebody vouch for you, as the oil combine vouched for us. Then at different, successive doorways you were scrutinized by a sequence of four uniformed guards, after which you were escorted to an elevator and lifted to the club's main dining room. From there, traveling on the coattails of the oil industry, you were led up a circular flight of stairs to the inner sanctum, the lounge, the playpen of the VIP's. And that's where we spent the evening.

It was plush, intimate, and delightful. The carpets were deep, the dance floor was highly polished, the fixtures were modern, the service was flawless.

A six-piece American dance band played music that was soft and rhythmic, led by a skillful pianist whose fingers wandered off into Chopin reveries between the sets. The lighting held just the right degree of low glow.

The ladies were friendly. Most of them were tastefully dressed in evening gowns and were sharing boredom with their husbands. The men were about equally divided between those wearing military uniforms and those in civilian dress. There were Scottish officers with kilts and sporrans, English officers with polished leather belts, French officers with great clusters of gold braid. I was the only American Navy officer present, a distinction which attracted frequent visitors to our table, offering the utmost in courtesy and charm.

For dinner we had consomme, a choice between salmon or trout, an excellent steak, a crisp salad, all with fine vintage wines, thick cubes of butter, rich cream, plenty of sugar, good coffee, and, finally, a choice of liqueur.

It was during our second cup of coffee that we heard the sound of planes passing overhead, and then in the distance the thump of gunfire. But that faded quickly, with nobody paying any attention to it. I wondered what happened at such moments to women who searched through garbage cans. Did they look for shelter or go on with their search?

From time to time strangers would join our party and would be introduced around by our oil combine hosts, until at last we had the largest table-gathering in the room, including a Scottish colonel in plaids, a Royal Navy commander, a Dutch diplomat, and anywhere from five to eight ladies, depending momentarily upon whether they felt like remaining or walking around.

And we all drank Scotch. Very good Scotch. Outside, all over Britain, it was being rationed at one bottle per family, per month. We began the evening with five bottles,

which seemed like a reasonable order since there was a
constant line of visitors from other tables, and it would
have been discourteous not to offer each visitor a drink.

Nobody seemed to care which lady paired off with
which gentleman, nor for how long, and it was the accepted thing to approach any table in the room to ask
anybody to dance or drink. A person who found himself
left alone for a moment had only to wander along to the
next party with, "Hello, there. Mind if I join you?" To
which might come, "Not at all, old chap. Will you enter-
tain my wife while I play a bit of poker?"

In some ways, the whole thing was like a new version
of the Alice-in-Wonderland tea party. Anybody, apparently, could do whatever he liked and be assured of
an enthusiastic, appreciative audience. The entire room
would rise and applaud any time a couple stopped dancing long enough to slide into a passionate embrace. The
applause was warm also for a French major who solemnly
stepped to the middle of the floor, gestured for attention,
stripped to the waist, and then stood on his head. The
ovation of the evening went to the Royal Navy commander from our table who moved into the spotlight,
drank a glass of whiskey "no hands" while holding it in
his teeth, and then slowly toppled over backward. We
picked him up and held him on his feet long enough for
him to bow to the applause, smile, and wave the whole
thing off with, "Nothing at all, nothing at all!" Then he
collapsed again.

We left the Piccadilly shortly before dawn and walked
back to the hotel. The rain by then had turned to a cold
drizzle. The streets were dark and wet and almost deserted. The shop window displays were meager and

shabby. Buildings along the way were badly in need of repair. Occasionally a shawled woman or a hunched man would shuffle along past us, eyes downcast toward the wet pavement, face pinched, perhaps hopeful at that early hour of being the first in line at some little food shop where a queue would be forming soon for thin rations of milk or bread or tea.

Glasgow looked as they had told us in New York it would look, beaten to its knees by the long months of war and sacrifice.

Back at the hotel, the sleepy desk clerk perked up with a knowing smile when we entered the lobby.

"Been to the Piccadilly, I hear?"

"That's right."

"Well now," he said, "there'll be no need to say Scotland's a dour country when you get home, will there?"

CHAPTER THIRTEEN

THE BATTERED BRITISH

A<small>N</small> UNUSUAL THING ABOUT MANY OF THE PORTS WE visited in England and Wales was that nothing about them seemed to be unusual. As we sailed in and out, up one coast and down another, month after month, they looked just about as we had expected them to look, and the people everywhere reacted just about as we had expected them to react.

Wherever we went, most of the people made friends with us. They had fought alone for so long, huddling together night after night when the bombs came down and going out hand-in-hand in the morning smoke, that the sight of somebody who had arrived to help them on toward victory seemed to give them new determination to keep on fighting. I suppose, too, that they felt particularly close to us because we were just ordinary gunners and seamen, little people like themselves. Sometimes we were in port with them for only two or three days, and at other times we might be with them for as long as three or four weeks. Regardless of time, we and the British became close friends, and we never sailed from any port but what there would be a knot of them or a crowd of them gathered at dockside to wave good-bye and to wish us a safe return.

When first we sailed into Swansea, edging *Gulfwing's*

long bulk through the narrow locks and canals that led in from the Bristol Channel, it was like revisiting a place that had long ago become familiar. That seemed strange, for none of us had been there before. Standing on the bridge, looking down at the piers and looking off at the hills, we wondered about it.

"I guess it's because of the movies," Tex said, leaning on the rail beside me. "This place is right out of *How Green Was My Valley*. In just a moment, we'll see Donald Crisp walking down past the church there, taking his son out to get into a fight and to learn what it's like to get a bloody nose."

He was right. It was the Green Valley town, grown to city size. The houses were all alike, running up the steep hillside to the mine pits. They looked drab and cheerless in the light rain that was falling. The hill that ranged along in back of the town was bright green in small patches, and dirty gray and black in bigger patches, where the slag and the coal dust lay thick upon the ground.

We walked the Swansea streets that afternoon, and we saw what a bad beating they had taken when German bombers had swooped in low over the hills and the coal pockets. We walked aimlessly for many blocks, and always there were ruins or rubble in one direction or another. The place was old and dirty and tired and grim, but it was not defeated. The people were shabbily dressed. Most of the women had no stockings. Most of the men were black-grimed miners, and the rest were idlers with dirty scarves around their throats, or they were Home Guard men in uniforms that didn't fit.

But all of them were friendly. When we sat with them at the bar in the Mackworth Hotel, and bought the house a round of ale, they accepted it with dignity; no apologies were ever offered or expected over the fact that they couldn't afford to buy a round in return.

They were a people who should have been rocking on their knees, beaten twice, once by life and once by war. But they would smile with you, and help you to find your way in the blacked-out streets at night. They would joke with you about what a surprise old Hitler was going to get one of these days. They would not, of course, give you any ice for your Scotch and soda, but after a time that ceased to be important.

Once when we were in Swansea it was Independence Day, and the newspapers were carrying a release from the Ministry of Information about the toll of submarine sinkings our convoy had scored on a previous trip across: ". . . four certainly, four almost certainly, and two probably." And then, in detail, came the score on the crossing we had just completed: "In a series of attacks extending over two days, one U-boat was destroyed, another probably destroyed, and others were damaged. A number of survivors from the U-boat were picked up by the destroyer H.M.S. *Escapade* and were made prisoners of war."

So, since it was the Fourth of July, and because we were feeling quite proud of our successes at sea, we dressed ship at sunrise, stringing all our multicolored signal flags along *Gulfwing's* rigging and superstructure, giving the dirt-stained waterfront probably the brightest display it had seen in many years. Before long, we saw a delegation plodding toward us from town, a stolid group of miners and shopkeepers who apparently had scrubbed hard to get the coal grime out of their pores and to look their best for the occasion of a visit to our ship.

They came aboard, and greeted us with much self-conscious clearing of throats.

"We are here," they said, "to pay our respects on the occurrence of your holiday, y'know. And we invite you to be our guests at the Mackworth for luncheon, in honor of General George Washington."

We went, and it was a wonderful treat. The best they could provide for luncheon was rabbit stew. But they also provided a warm friendliness made up of songs and toasts and cheers for the Navy and the merchant marine that made it an unforgettable Independence Day away from home.

One of the biggest problems an American had in Swansea lay not in trying to get along with the townsfolk but in trying to get a good shave or haircut ashore. All of the barber shops were dirty, bare little places set in the back room of a tobacco store or a stationer's shop or a newsdealer's establishment. They all used old, tobacco-stained armchairs with no lift. They all drew their hot water from a steam kettle on a gas range. They all used the same towel for every customer. Not one of them had an electric clipper. The best and safest thing to ask for was a quick trim with the hope of an early getaway.

The one barber shop that looked interesting to us was at the back of a tobacco store down a side alley, but none of us had the nerve to try it. We were frightened away by the sign outside, a wide, chalked blackboard that read:

"The Great Vitosky—America's Greatest Hairdresser—Get a Smashing Haircut from the Great Vitosky—The Great Polish Hairdresser— Mexico City's Greatest Hair Artist—Shoe Laces

For Sale Today—Known from Butte, Montana, to Miami, Florida—Known from Fort Worth to Boston—Little Pots for Children, For Sale Here —Vitosky is the Greatest Barber in the Empire —Vitosky is South Africa's Great Wonder Hairdresser—Get Your Hair Cut Here and Tell the World Vitosky Did It—California's Sunkist Polish Barber—Fish Hooks and Hair Pins on Special Sale."

Reading all that, we decided there was no telling what Vitosky might do if he got a man's head in one hand and a razor or a pair of shears in the other. So we passed him by.

But when at last we sailed from Swansea, the Great Vitosky was right there with the crowd at dockside, holding no rancor, busily passing out his business cards to liberty parties as they returned to ship from their last farewells in town.

"Come back soon!" he called out as we moved away from the pier. "Vitosky never forgets a friend!"

That was what we were afraid of.

Upon leaving Swansea, we usually stopped off for a convoy conference at Milford Haven, a short sail up the west coast of Wales. It was as charming a place as Swansea was drab. It made you think of Cape Cod, with its bright sands, clean beaches, green meadows, and low-flying seagulls.

On we would go to Liverpool, usually into the Herculaneum Docks. Liverpool was so shabby, so wrecked, and so depressing in those days that most Armed Guard crews prayed not to be sent there, and when they did enter the

mouth of the Mersey River and caught sight of the gro-
tesque Liver Bird brooding over what was left of the city,
its burned-out shells of buildings, its shoddy streets, its
acres and acres of war scars, they prayed for a quick turn-
around and an early departure.

I had friends in Liverpool, though, friends and distant
relatives, living in a suburb called Upton, across the river
from the downtown city. From time to time I found myself going there by train, when our ship lay in some other
port that would have been far more comfortable and
entertaining.

One such trip came when we were tied up in Morecambe Bay, a clean and restful part of England with rich
green fields and quiet beaches. I caught a seven-forty
train out of Morecambe Promenade Station on a Saturday
evening, heading south on the London, Midlands and
Scottish Railway. At Lancaster, where I had to change
trains and where I was beginning to feel hot and thirsty,
the station pub had long since run out of beer and ale.
So I sat there drinking weak tea and feeling sorry for
myself.

But as I've said, there were friendly people everywhere
in those days. I was working on my second cup of tea
when two old Irish women staggered in from the darkened street, politely drunk, and hiccuped their way to my
table. From somewhere beneath their skirts, they produced two bottles of Guinness and placed them carefully
on the table in front of me.

"Askin' your pardon," they croaked, "but it's not a fit
drink you're drinkin'."

"You're right," I said, "but it's all they have here."

"Well now," they said, "as we looked in through the

window and took you for a gentleman, we thought you might share the use of the Guinness here with the two of us."

"It would be my pleasure," I said.

"More like it would be our pleasure," they said, "but we've not got the time for it. We've a boat to catch now, to sail back to Ireland. So we leave you our Guinness and God's blessing, and please to enjoy them both."

With that, they hiccuped back out to the street again, and moved off uncertainly in the general direction of the waterfront.

The two bottles of Guinness lasted me until the train for Preston came in, and from there to Liverpool I enjoyed the ride immensely. The moon was full. The countryside and villages were completely blacked out, but the little lanes and canals and farms and cottages stood out like toy pieces in a dimly-lighted show window. Even the herds of cows and the flocks of sheep were clearly discernible in the meadows as we rolled along.

We arrived at Liverpool's Exchange Station shortly after midnight, and going out into Lime Street was like stepping into a city of the dead. The moon had slunk behind clouds by then, peering out only occasionally to reflect against the gaunt, jagged ruins of the bombed buildings.

I remembered other nights in Liverpool when there had been crowded drinking parties at the Hotel Adelphi, when there had been bombers overhead, when there had been fires in the streets. But now the streets were wholly deserted, and there wasn't a glimmer of light visible from behind door cracks or window shades or blackout curtains. There was nobody in sight, just nobody. I stopped and listened, and in that entire great city I could hear no sound louder than my own breathing.

I had expected to cross the river and to be in Upton by midnight, but the trains had been running late, and now it looked as though I might not get there until morning. The subway train under the Mersey had stopped running for the night. There wasn't a taxi to be had, nor a telephone from which to call one. So I walked off in what I thought was the general direction of the river, hoping to catch a late boat across. Somewhere along the dark streets, I fell in with an Australian soldier who was trying to overcome the same problem I had. So together we finally found the docks just in time to get aboard the last ferry for Birkenhead on the opposite side of the Mersey.

At Birkenhead, the streets were just as dark, but they were not deserted, not at least at the ferry landing. There were a dozen people standing there waiting for a taxi, and some of them had been stranded for more than an hour.

I left them, and walked around until I came to a policeman and told him my problem. He said he liked Americans reasonably well, and since it was much too far to walk to Upton he'd find a taxi for me.

He did. He stopped an Austin that already had six passengers riding inside, and he told the hunchback driver to make room for me on the front seat.

I still don't know how it was accomplished but they managed to fit me in, complete with gas mask and musette bag. I was driven around the countryside until two o'clock in the morning, by which time all the other passengers had been dropped off at their individual stops. When the last of them had gone, I told the little hunchback driver to pull off to the side of the road, and I took a bottle of Scotch out of my musette bag and opened some fresh cigarettes, and we sat there enjoying several drinks together while we told each other various lies about the war.

Shortly before dawn, he delivered me at my Upton destination, and I stepped out and thanked him and reached for my billfold and asked: "How much is all that?"

He glared at me. "You deserve a punch in the face for asking," he said. "Put it away." And he slipped his car into gear and raced off, with his rear tires kicking up a shower of gravel.

We sometimes docked at Heysham, and other times at Blackpool, to wait for other ships to join us. And everywhere there were always the friendly people, the battered people, the people who had taken more of a war-pounding than anyone should have to stand, but who had never lost their courage or their sense of humor.

They even ridiculed themselves in song, making light of their troubles. A crack-voiced tenor weighed duty against desperation in a Blackpool music hall one night with a song about the awkward difficulties of trying to spot enemy aircraft from a lookout perch where the seagulls were active:

> Spotting on the top of Blackpool Tower
> When the evening sun is low,
> There you'll find me hour after hour
> While seagulls up above
> Drop messages of love.
> Last night one came swoopin' down

As I lay on my bed,
I called all the guns in town
To shoot the bahstard dead;
But 'e flew in and scored a 'it
Directly on my 'ead,
Spotting on the top of Blackpool Tower.

And then there were the Londoners, all the wonderful people in that big, sprawling, dirty, smoky, foggy, damp, gray, bomb-scarred, tremendous city.

We approached London from the Channel and from E-boat alley on a dark, cold day, and we turned in at the mouth of the Thames in the middle of a bitter snow and sleet squall. We moved on up-river, past dozens of wrecks and sunken hulks, past the skeleton-like fingers of masts poking out of the water, past the ugly antiaircraft towers with their iron and concrete gun emplacements, anchored in the bed of the dirty stream. Then we dropped our hook at Gravesend for an overnight stay, and we stood by the rail and watched the people on the passing tug boats and barges, all wearing life jackets, all with gas masks slung over their shoulders.

At midnight, a tug came alongside and tied up to us, to sit there and wait for the turn of the morning tide before pushing us farther up the river. It was so dark there in that midstream blackout that we never did see the tug from our own bridge, but we could hear its quiet hissing and creaking somewhere below, and the occasional ripe cursing of some deckhand down there, bumping his shins in the blackness. At dawn we moved on to the East End waterfront and to the Royal Albert docks, where we tied up to make our home for two weeks.

London, on that visit, was a ten-night string of violent air raids, huge fires, and what was described in Parliament as "the biggest antiaircraft barrage of the war."

But it was much else. For one thing, it was the contagious bravery and nonchalance of the Londoner.

There was the night, for example, when we were drinking at the American Bar in the Savoy, and the planes of the *Luftwaffe* came roaring over in a heavy attack that rocked the whole heart of the city and turned the night into a wild din. As we hurried to leave and get back to our ship, we paused abruptly on our way through the lobby to see the hotel manager calmly putting up a sign on the functions board.

Very soon, he had the whole thing arranged neatly in place. It read, for all to notice: "Air Raid Now in Progress."

And equally nonchalant were the two old gentlemen who rode with me on a bus one night when another air attack was hammering the city. Our bus somehow was making its way down toward Aldgate East, past raging fires and slamming guns. It was a night of death, noise, and destruction, but the bus was keeping strictly to its schedule, and the two old gentlemen were riding along and occasionally glancing out the window, as though only mildly interested in the flaming clatter outside.

Then one of them leaned across the aisle and tapped me on my uniform sleeve.

"You're a Yankee, sir. Am I right?" he asked.

"Yes," I said. "That's right."

"This is our 709th raid." He beamed, proud as a new father.

"Who counts them?" I asked.

"Oh, we all do!" he said. "Been doing it for years, y'know. Quite a good one tonight."

It seemed an odd thing to say, in view of the obvious fact that London was taking a savage beating, that fires were scourging whole neighborhoods, that from time to time the walls of blazing buildings were collapsing in great mushrooms of flame and debris.

At about that moment, there was a tremendous crash behind us as a German bomber plunged into the street and showered the area with its burning wreckage.

This time the other old gentleman leaned across and tapped me. "Giving 'em 'ell tonight, are we not?"

You had to like and admire a people like that, and knowing how London reacted under pressure, you never again thought of the city as anything less than great.

London in wartime, as a port of call for convoy ships, was an endless parade of unforgettable impressions. It was the bomb-pocked statue of Richard Coeur de Lion, and the floating mines in the muddy current of the Thames. It was the whores of Piccadilly at night, and the drunks asleep on the pavements of Soho at dawn. It was the Grosvenor, where 3,000 American officers ate together every evening. And it was Billingsgate, where the air was filled with the smell of fish, and where the surplus mussels and periwinkles left over from the day's sales cluttered the gutters at sundown.

It was Limehouse in a blackout, when the only sound you could hear would be the voice of some unseen, home-sick American walking along and singing "The Whiffen-poof Song." It was Trafalgar Square, with the soldiers standing in line to be photographed feeding the pigeons. It was Leicester Square, with its bookstalls filled with pornography. It was Waterloo Bridge with its street-walkers, and Big Ben bonging a somber, reassuring tone in the fog, and the crowds staring at the bomb-smashed corner of St. James Palace. It was jugged hare and wine at Simpson's-in-the-Strand, and a warm rabbit pie at the King's Head. It was a thick tangle of barbed wire on Downing Street, to halt the Germans if they got that far. It was the bravery of spirit that could decide to place machine gun nests around Nelson's Statue, camouflage them to look like shuttered news stands, and then chuckle to think of what a surprise the German troops would get when they gathered there to go sightseeing.

London in those days was a cloud of barrage balloons, floating around like bloated, airborne pigs. It was the Windmill Theater running its nightly show of nudes no matter how many bombs came crashing down. It was the welcome you got as an American when you went pub-crawling, and when you were greeted with so many toasts from old men and old women that if you could have saved them all you could have floated a landing craft.

London also was the brutal ugliness of war; the young men with one leg or one arm or blind; the family group standing in a smoking dawn and looking sadly at the ruins of their home; the sorrowful women weeping in the churches; the mothers and fathers waiting in patient resignation while rescue workers dug into the ruins of a bombed flat for the bodies of dead little girls and boys.

And as much as anything, I suppose, London was the elderly fire warden at the Royal Albert Docks who asked permission to come aboard my ship one night during a heavy raid. The bombers were roaring overhead, the flak was ripping the sky, and the Thames tide was red with fire reflections, when he came up to me on the ship's bridge, with his helmet set squarely on his head, and his mouth quivering a little with emotion. He was well past middle age. He should not have had to be going through blows of violence at his time of life.

He wanted to ask my permission to fire one of our 20-millimeter guns.

"You see, sir," he explained, "they got my family and my home in last night's raid. They're all gone now, all dead. And everything is gone. And ten of my good friends, they're gone too. I just want the chance to shoot back, if it's not asking too much. For my family and my home and my good friends."

I gave him the chance. I took one of my men from his gun and let the old fire warden use it, and I felt glad for him as he stood there with a thin smile on his face, with his fingers on the trigger, slamming the shells high into the sky at the enemy planes overhead.

He may not have hit anything. But he had earned the right to try.

CHAPTER FOURTEEN

THE LAND OF WIND

O N A COLD, WET FEBRUARY MORNING, WE SAT ABOARD
ship in London awaiting our sailing orders and
feeling hopefully confident that they would read: "Destination, New York."

We had been on the wrong side of the Atlantic for a
long time. There seemed to be no reason to stick around
any longer. All of our cargo had been discharged, our
thousands of tons of bombs and shells and our dozens of
tanks. Most of it was still sitting out there alongside the
dock in stacked rows that glistened under the midwinter
rain. Our ship rode high and light and empty, rolling
gently on the Thames tide, and we were talking about the
fact that it would be necessary to take ballast aboard
before moving out to fight the North Atlantic gales on a
westward crossing.

Then a WREN came aboard with our orders. They
read: "Destination, Reykjavik." Our new assignment, we
learned, was to sail to Iceland, to take on a full cargo of
thousands of tons of explosives from the Army and Navy
ammunition dumps there, and to bring the whole load back
to England, to be added to the huge invasion stockpiles.

The convoy conference for that voyage was held at
Methil, on the Firth of Forth, and it was as cheerless as

139

convoy conferences invariably seemed to be when they were held in British ports.

That was something that always puzzled us—the difference in the atmosphere of a convoy conference in a United States or a Canadian port, and the same type of a convoy conference anywhere in the United Kingdom.

The personnel makeup was always the same, with the merchant captains and the Armed Guard commanding officers sitting together while some Admiral in charge introduced the Escort Commander and the Convoy Commodore, and outlined the routes, destinations, and special emergency tactics.

In New York or Boston or Norfolk or Halifax, there was an electricity to those conferences. They were held in well-lighted surroundings, amidst great wall maps and marine charts, where mock-up convoy formations were moved about and where late reports on the location of submarine wolfpacks were illustrated by lights and models. When you left to return to ship and await departure time, you went out feeling the way a well-trained football team does when it runs from the locker room onto the playing field for the start of the second half. You felt alive and confident and ready for hard action.

In British ports, though, the convoy conferences almost always were held in some dark and depressing backroom down a waterfront side street. There you sat, in a cloud of thick tobacco smoke, drinking lukewarm tea, watching the rain stream down the dirty window panes, staring at bare patches where green paint had peeled from the walls, and trying to pay attention to the Royal Navy Admiral in charge as he mumbled his instructions and information in a monotone that nearly put everybody to sleep. When you left, you felt drowsy and lethargic and indifferent.

That was the kind of a conference we had at Methil. We could sense right away that this was not going to be a happy voyage.

There were only six merchant ships listed for the Reykjavik run. Two of us were American Liberty ships, two were British vessels of about 10,000 tons, one was a Greek freighter, and one was a small Icelandic ship. We were assigned three escorts.

Our ship was chosen for the Vice Commodore assignment, and one of the British freighters drew the role of Commodore ship. And that's when trouble began.

"Commodore or not," said the skipper of the British freighter, "I do not care to go. My ship is tired, my crew is tired. We are unfit to sail to Iceland, even if conditions were good. To attempt such a voyage now, in the face of midwinter arctic gales and hostile Jerries, would be asinine. Especially since you're asking us to bring back munitions. I'll have none of it." He sat back defiantly, puffing away on his pipe.

The admiral in charge of the conference stared at him coldly from beneath raised eyebrows. "You, sir," he said, "will go to Reykjavik in convoy. And you, sir, will go as the Commodore ship. And I'll not listen to any further discussion."

The British skipper mumbled something under his breath that sounded like, "You can bloody well take it and ——" something or other. Then the conference broke up. Going out, I had the strong feeling that we were soon to move up from Vice Commodore to Commodore for this particular voyage.

I was right. We all sailed from Methil to Loch Ewe

and waited there for two days in a slashing snowstorm. It cleared on the morning of the third day, and shortly before dawn the Royal Navy station on shore flashed the signal for our departure. The winches groaned and the anchor chains rattled. We stood on the bridge watching the Commodore ship, waiting for the reluctant British skipper to get under way and to lead the rest of us out to sea.

He got under way without difficulty. But then he made the shortest voyage I had ever seen a convoy ship complete. As soon as he began to move, to our shocked astonishment, he ran up his black-ball "Out of Control" signal, swung hard right, and rammed his bow squarely into the side of the American freighter. Then he promptly dropped anchor and ended his trip right there. The stunned American was abruptly knocked out of business too, with a fair-sized gash in her hull just above the water line. But the British skipper had won his point—Reykjavik was not for him.

That incident automatically moved our ship into the Commodore role, and so off we went, leaving the two cripples behind us. Our little fleet steamed out of Loch Ewe and pointed toward the wild and wintry arctic—one American ship, one British, one Greek, one Icelandic, and the nondescript escorts.

We were the only ship carrying weapons that were worth anything. The Icelander had nothing with which to fight off submarines and aircraft, although through the glasses I could see that her captain wore a pistol in a holster. The Greek had two 30-caliber machine guns mounted on the bridge. The remaining British skipper carried 50-caliber machine guns on his bridge and some sort of a gun under heavy canvas on his stern, but since he never removed the lashed tarpaulin that hid it we never could determine what it was.

Our three escorts were nothing but small Royal Navy trawlers, each carrying only two 20-millimeter guns and a two-inch bow gun.

But on our ship, we were armed with eight 20-millimeter guns, plus a dependable 4"/50 at the stern, plus a 3"/50 dual purpose gun at the bow, all in the hands of an experienced gun crew that knew how to react to any kind of attack. Suddenly, we felt we were in the unique position of escorting the escorts.

It took us more than a week to make the journey. Wild gales and submarine action off the Faeroe Islands drove us far off our course and northeast toward the Arctic Circle before we eluded the U-boats and swung westward toward Iceland. We finally arrived at Reykjavik without a casualty, moving in on a March dawn, gliding across a glassy sea under an arctic sky that somehow gave us the feeling of sailing through a cavern beneath a vast purple dome. The lights of Icelandic fishing vessels gleamed across the dark water as we approached, and they looked like white globes dangling on a Christmas tree, or like stars that had dropped part way down from the dark canopy overhead and were hanging quietly and without motion just above the water. It was very still and very weird, like sailing into another world. The moaning wind cried out with an eerie sound that never quite went away.

As the sun rose, its red light flickered across ice caps and glacier fields on the shore, and reflected down the sides of rugged cliffs that reached to the sea. It shone, too, on black volcanic rock, drifted over with patches of deep snow.

We stayed in Reykjavik for ten days while the military stevedore gangs crammed our holds with high explosives, and lashed dozens of tanks and PT-boats to the open decks. In all those ten days, we never had a monotonous hour.

The Army entertained us at dinner at Camp Haggi, and then took us to the Army Officers Club for drinks and conversation. The Navy entertained us at Camp Knox, and then took us to the Navy Officers Club for more of the same. For the gunners and seamen, the services opened up all the recreational facilities of the base, making possible football and baseball in the snow, boxing and tennis in the gymnasium, swimming in a pool made warm by hot, volcanic waters, and climbing from the pool to dive into ten-foot snowdrifts. Always there was the wind, with its haunting, eerie sound that never went away, and always there was the unreal beauty of Reykjavik after dark, with snow falling heavily through the uneasy air, with the lights in the shop windows glowing all night.

We arranged on one clear day for a Navy truck to take us high up into the mountains for a day of skiing. When the truck arrived at dockside early the next morning, another snowstorm already had begun. Nevertheless, we drove off through the swirling flakes, far out beyond the city, up into a region where lava peaks and volcanic crevasses made a fantastic, snowcapped jumble of the scenery. We spent all day out there, using a mountain hut that was well stocked with firewood and food, skiing down the steep slopes and sometimes falling into deep drifts, climbing laboriously up the tall mountain sides and then

rushing down again headlong with the rising storm whipping at our faces.

All day long the storm kept on and the wind grew
stronger, so we decided about four o'clock in the afternoon
that it was time to head back before the mounting drifts
closed all the roads and passes and left us snowed-in for
a week or more.

We barely made it at that, and only after being lost
and marooned for two hours. The storm by then had
whipped itself into an arctic blizzard, and the temperature had plunged down to around zero. The wind was
blowing at a hurricane force of close to ninety miles an
hour. We tried to fight our way down the mountainside
with the truck, only to find that the drifts already had
blocked the main road out and were piling higher every
minute.

We backed off, then, and hunted around among the
passes until we found another road, and even as we came
upon it, the storm was building yet another drift to block
our way. The only thing to do was to jump from the
truck and break the drift apart to open a way through.
By then, it was so bitterly cold and the wind was blowing
with such fury, that as the gunners leaped from inside
the truck, their faces turned dark brown almost before
they could hit the ground and dash around to the front.
Instant snow-tan, something none of us had ever seen
before.

In the end, we broke clear of the mountains after dark
and got back on the main road to Reykjavik before any
more drifts could block our route. The snow-tans lasted
about twenty-four hours, and then disappeared.

Reykjavik on that visit was like a city that was outside

the warring world, and somehow had managed to wrap itself in seclusion. It seemed strange to walk along past the bright shop windows at night, and to stare at refrigerators and electric flatirons and thick sides of beef, and all the good things that had not been on general sale back in the states for many months. It seemed ridiculous to enter a store, hoping to buy a bottle of Scotch, only to discover it was selling for $30 a fifth, and so to settle instead for an ice cream soda farther down the street. It was a moving experience to stand on deck at night and watch the Northern Lights wave and sparkle overhead, reflecting their colored ribbons of light on the dark waters of Reykjavik Harbor. It was an unforgettable sight to watch the storms come whirling down from the lava mountains in great cyclones of black clouds and blown snow.

All in all, it was a visit to remember—to remember, but not to repeat. There was a maddening effect in the way the wind never stopped blowing, and in having to listen to its sad moaning hour after hour, day and night. The wind did something to a man's mind. It crept inside, somehow, and fed upon normal reasoning, and slowly ate at the brain. It was something too remote and strange and unreal for the average Yankee mind to put up with for long spells of time.

And in some cases, it drove men crazy. It made a maniac of an Army sentry who was walking his post one night, listening to the ever-present wind. He turned aside for a moment, stepped into a Quonset hut where his commanding officer was asleep, and put a bullet into the man's head. Then he returned to the slow, quiet pacing of his post outside.

It drove others crazy too, the loneliness and the snow

and the moaning of the wind that never went away, and some of them were shipped out to stateside hospitals, and others ran amok before their sickness was discovered.

If you had talked recently to normal people in London or New York, and then talked to the men who had spent many months in Iceland, it was easy to tell there was something wrong with them. Fortunately, most of them got over it in time, and perhaps never even realized what had happened to them. But others could never understand why it was not perfectly all right to kill a man in his bed; it relieved the monotony, and perhaps it might stop the sound of the wind when nothing else seemed to work.

When at last we sailed away, no Reykjavik townsfolk came down to the shore to see us off. For ten days, they had been looking through us as though we were not there. In all that time, they had seemed to be saying to themselves that some day all this would pass, the war would end, the strangers would go away, and then they could be alone again, alone with their storms and their lights and their constant, moaning wind.

CHAPTER FIFTEEN

WEIRD AND UNKNOWN

T HE WINDS OF ICELAND WERE NOT THE ONLY STRANGE, uncanny things that have lived in memory through the years, and that come back now to haunt the recall of the convoy days. There were other things, other visitations, that were even stranger and sometimes more chilling, and that seem as vivid and unreal now as they did at the moment of their happening. We heard them or saw them or felt them, as surely as we heard the crack of thunder in a tropical hurricane or saw the rising of an African moon or felt the stinging whip of an arctic gale, and yet they seemed in some cases to be from an unnatural world that did not recognize our normal order of things.

Who can ever say, for example, what force created and controlled the balls of cold light that appeared suddenly above our ships one still March night as we sailed near the Arctic Circle, and that stayed with us for a full hour, following our changes of course, and then suddenly swung high into the sky above us and sped off in formation, vanishing toward the polar cap.

They were not reflections or hallucinations or mirages or freaks of vision seen by only one or two weary men on watch. They were real balls of light, four of them, that appeared overhead without warning where the sky had

148

been black and impenetrable, and that hung somewhere between the zenith and the mast tops of our little four-ship convoy with its three escorts. It was impossible to tell just how high they hung, for there was no way of gauging a perspective against the dark sky and, therefore, no way of telling how big they were.

We were in the waters of the Norwegian Sea at the time, for while en route to Iceland we had been forced far north of our planned course and into a lonely part of the world where ships seldom strayed. It was a black night, with high clouds shutting out the stars, and up until well after midnight we had been content with having it stay all black and lonely; that meant that the submarines had lost us, and that we were alone but safe for the time being in a sea of soft sounds and cold darkness, making swift but quiet headway.

Then suddenly they were there, four identical balls of light, appearing abruptly overhead in about the same relative positions as the four ships in formation below. They looked cold and white. They did not glisten or sparkle or gleam. They just hung there in the sky like pale, white, watching globes.

I was on the bridge at the time, wearing the battle-phones, and I heard several lookout-gunners starting to call in at once, but the voice from the forward gun was just an instant ahead of the others.

"Three-inch to bridge."

"Yes," I said. "I see them."

"Three-inch to bridge. What are they?" The gunner's voice was tight and nervous.

"I don't know."

We watched them in wary silence. They stayed with

us, hanging poised and cold against the blackness over-head.

We were the Commodore ship and we were respon-sible for the others, and so we blinked the order for a sudden course change, forty-five degrees to port. The ships swung around in formation, and our escort craft came swinging around with us, and we all straightened out on the new compass bearing and sailed silently off toward the south, thinking to leave the lights behind.

But the lights swung too, holding their position di-rectly overhead.

After a while we changed course again, forty-five degrees to starboard. The strange lights stayed right along with us, maintaining speed and never wavering from their fixed locations.

On the bridge of our ship, looking across the water, we caught sight of the flickering red glow of an Aldis signal lamp as a call came our way from one of the other con-voy ships. We acknowledged with our own Aldis, knowing that it would shut out our signal beam from any viewer except the one who had called us.

We knew what the query would be, even before it came glimmering at us across the waves: "What are they?"

"Do not know," we flickered back. "Hold formation. Regard as friendly."

If they were not friendly, at least they were not hostile. They made no move to descend or to approach us. They simply stayed there, hanging in the night sky, riding along above us for a full hour as we sailed on our way through the dark arctic waters, maintaining our silence and our speed and our uneasy watchfulness. All the time, our guns were held trained on the strange balls of light. And all the time, we hoped we would not have to shoot at them.

As it happened, we did not. Shortly before two o'clock in the morning, the light balls suddenly began to recede upward, all four moving at once as though on signal, pulling away from their positions to higher and higher altitudes at a speed that was astonishing. And then, poised high overhead, they streaked off toward the north and within moments had vanished from sight.

Their departure left us relieved but shaken. We never did know what they were, where they came from, what they sought, or where they went.

How does one explain a thing like that, except to point out that it happened at sea, and that the sea contains many mysteries, and always will?

And how does one explain the castle that vanished in Ireland? We saw it. It was there in the mist, with its dead watch-holes looking out to sea. But when we looked for it again, it was gone. And it never returned.

The one time we saw it was on an April evening, when we were nearing the end of a long Atlantic voyage, and had finally put the heaving waves of the open sea behind us. We moved into North Channel, past Rathlin Island and Ballycastle, with the mountains of Antrim visible on our right and the dark, green peninsula of Argyll on our left.

We turned south, following close in along the coast of Ireland, as Scotland fell away to port. The twilight was thick with a heavy mist, but not so thick as to obscure the Irish shore. On the contrary, its wetness gave a vivid strength to the colors of the countryside, and we could see clearly the bright greens and the dark browns and the whitish grays of the farms and lanes and empty fields and rocky beaches. It was a haunting scene, unforgettable in its melancholy beauty and its colors and shadows. We leaned on the starboard rail, watching in silence as the ship moved along on the gentle sea.

Then, somewhere before we made the turn into Belfast Lough, we saw it come into view—a gaunt castle that stood high in its own stone ruins, a castle on a flat spit of land with nothing around but fields of dark green and the foaming white of the waves on shore. It looked like a relic of centuries, with its rock walls streaked with moss and with its high sentry-holes gaping like dead, empty eyes.

We stared at it in fascination as we passed close by, and then we looked back at it as the ship moved along and the castle grew smaller in the distance, until at last it was gone from sight, hidden in the mist that overhung the shore.

Nobody said anything for a long time. Then a gunner, leaning on the rail at my left, said quietly: "I don't re-member that castle from the last time we came this way."

"No," I said.

"It wasn't there, was it?"

"No." I shook my head. "Last time, there was nothing there at all."

In the eighteen months that followed, some of us passed that way at least six times, and we always looked for it, but we never saw the castle again. Where it had been, we never again saw anything but grass.

We could find no logical explanation for the vanishing castle, or for the strange arctic lights, or for some of the other uncanny experiences that took place later. But for one of the visitations, unusual as it was, there was a simple answer—St. Elmo's Fire.

In the prosaic words of the dictionary, St. Elmo's Fire is a corposant—"A light due to atmospheric electricity, sometimes seen on the mastheads and yard-arms of ships." And Richard Dana, when he wrote *Two Years Before the Mast,* pointed out that: "Sailors have a notion that if the corposant rises in the rigging, it is a sign of fair weather, but if it comes lower down, there will be a storm."

Our gunners on *Gulfwing* had no such notion, for as it turned out not one of them had ever heard of this eerie phenomenon. That was not surprising, for some mariners spend a lifetime at sea and never catch sight of its flame.

As for coming "lower down," if our St. Elmo's Fire had chosen to come aboard at a point much lower than it did, it would have been throwing its flame at our ammunition stores.

We met this fascinating freak of nature on an August midnight, as we were running alone up the Irish Sea, heading north for the Clyde to join a westbound convoy. We had been through two days of intermittent electric storms. The sea that night had a rolling swell, but still we were making good time, running blacked-out through the hot, sticky night. The rain had been falling all through the afternoon and evening, but now it had stopped. The sky seemed to hang low. The world seemed pitch-black except for quick flashes of lightning that kept wavering along the horizon.

I was in the charthouse, checking the day's run and trying to estimate the next day's time of arrival when, suddenly, a lookout-gunner came bursting in from the bridge, his face dead white with alarm.

"Lieutenant! Quick! The three-inch gun's on fire!"

I thought he had gone crazy, but I dashed out and stared forward. I took one look at the incredible sight of a flame dancing wildly on the gun barrel, and then I scrambled toward it as fast as I could move.

Halfway there, it dawned on me what was happening, and I checked my rush. What we were seeing was a rare display of St. Elmo's Fire on one of its unannounced visits. This was something to cherish for memory, not to view with alarm.

I made my way up to the gun deck, where the two forward lookouts were staring at the afflicted weapon as though they couldn't believe their eyes.

A tongue of bright-colored, electric flame, varying from twelve to eighteen inches tall, was spurting up from the tip of the gun's elevated barrel, waving back and forth like an excited cobra. As we watched, a second flame, about eight inches long, shot out from the side of the barrel, writhing at right angles to the taller one. The entire length of the gun gave out a noise that crackled and hummed and hissed.

The display lasted for several moments. Then suddenly—zip!—the flames vanished and the noise stopped. We were in total darkness again, with no sound but the rush of the sea at *Gulfwing's* bow, and no lights to be seen but the distant flashes on the horizon.

I put my hand on the gun barrel, and it felt cool, as though nothing had happened there. But we knew we had just seen an electric fire, and we were aware of the fact that we carried twenty-four high explosive fuse shells in the ready box just behind the gun, and none of us wanted to risk an outbreak of fire-dancing at that spot.

So we put a rubber tarpaulin over the metal ammunition box, and trusted to chance that St. Elmo was through for the night.

I doubt that the forward lookouts were of much value to us for the next few hours. I don't think they took their eyes away from the gun barrel until they went off watch.

St. Elmo's display could be explained. It was startling but it was natural. All it really meant, I suppose, was that old St. Erasmus had taken us under his protection, and had sent the Elmo flame to let us know.

There were other strange incidents for which we never found an answer. Sometimes they were incidents that left us with a shivery feeling, for there was nothing natural about them.

We never could explain, for instance, the sound of the singing voice that came softly but clearly over the ship's battlephones. There can be a reason for a strange voice on a telephone or on a radio receiver, but not on a ship's battlephone system. The battlephones we carried were sound-powered. They created their own energy from the sound vibrations that went into the open mouthpiece at any one of the eleven transmitting points on the system. By standing on the ship's bridge and looking around in a full circle, you could bring every one of those points into view. Our battlephones had no natural or mechanical connection whatever, in any way, with the world that lay beyond our open decks.

And yet, one night off the coast of Tunis, listening on the phones, we heard the soft, sweet voice of a woman singing an Arabic song. There were six men standing lookout by their guns at the time, and a petty officer in charge of the watch was standing beside me on the bridge wearing his phones. It was a quiet, starlit night, and there was little to report. Sometimes half an hour would pass without a word being spoken over the phone system. It was a good night for silence and smooth cruising.

And then, moving into that silence, came the voice of the singing woman.

The petty officer, listening to the first notes, thought one of his men was trying to be funny.

"Knock it off," he growled into his mouthpiece. "Pay attention to your job."

The soft singing went on.

"Knock it off yourself," came back from one of the lookouts. "Which one of us do you think can sing like that?"

After that, we all listened in silence. The song went on for several moments, rising and falling in faint but clear tones. We thought it might be coming across the water from land, or from some darkened boat between us and the shore. But when we took off our phones to listen, we could hear nothing. The singing was in the battlephone system and nowhere else and, yet, that was impossible.

After a while, it stopped. It did not fade away, and it did not break off in the middle of a tonal phrase. The gentle voice simply came to the end of its song and then was heard no more.

Nobody ever could explain why we heard it at all.

Such things remain mysteries.

So, too, does the colossal migration of jellyfish into which we plowed one day in the cold, northern waters off the coast of Greenland.

There were millions upon millions of them and they clogged the sea for many miles in a blue-gray gelatinous mass that seemed almost thick enough to walk upon. We sailed through them for more than thirty hours, during which time thousands of them even found their way to our decks and lay there shimmering in the sunlight by day, or lying there like dark slime at night, while we grew weary of pushing them back into the sea. We were completely puzzled as to where this gigantic migration was heading and why at that time of the year, for it was so late in the fall that we were already at the cold edge of winter, and yet these creatures were stubbornly pushing themselves straight into the frigid north. Granted that neither temperature nor direction probably means much to a jellyfish, it still seemed a strange course to be taking at that particular season.

After a while we ran out of them. We estimated they had covered an area close to 400 miles long and at least ten miles wide.

Then, too, there was the mystery of the plunging barometer. We encountered that experience in near-perfect weather in mid-Atlantic on a warm summer day when the sun was bright and the sea was smooth and there was not a cloud to be seen in the sky. The bridge barometer had been standing for hours at a normal high-pressure 30-degree reading, an ideal level for the ideal weather in which we were sailing.

Then suddenly it started down, slowly at first and then gaining speed, dropping degree by degree until it reached a low-pressure reading that was fit only for an extremely violent storm. We watched in astonishment as it hit an unbelievable low at the 26-degree mark, while the weather all around remained at midsummer perfection, and never a hostile breeze fanned the sea.

Then back it climbed, up and up, degree by degree, until at last it reached its original level at the 30-degree mark, and there it stayed.

The whole process had taken about two hours. But what had happened in those two hours?—what strange atmospheric freak had we sailed through? We never knew.

Nor did we ever know the identity of the tremendous sea beast that we struck one night in midocean. Whatever it was, it must have been lurking just below the surface, for as we cruised along in the darkness at just under ten knots our keel suddenly jarred into some unknown body with such force that the entire ship shook from bow to stern. For an instant we felt ourselves lifted a foot or more above our cruising level, and then dropped back with a lurching shiver. And there was something about the feel of the collision and the rushing swirl of water that followed, that told us unmistakably that, whatever it was we had hit, it was not a thing of metal or wood, but was a living thing, an enormous living thing, large enough to move a ship of 10,000 tons.

We never learned the answers to those strange experiences and visitations. And now, of course, we never will.

CHAPTER SIXTEEN

UNDER PRESSURE

SOMETIMES WHEN PRESSURE BUILDS INSIDE A MAN AT sea, and when his nerves or his mind may be nearing the breaking point, you can read the slow buildup as clearly as you can read the pressure gauge on an engine-room boiler. You can see it in the man's eyes, or in the twitching of his mouth, or in the growing tautness of his voice, and then you have time to plan what to do when the explosion comes.

Sometimes, with other men, there is no way of knowing that the buildup is taking place, for they keep their emotions locked inside themselves and there is no tell-tale indicator. When the explosion comes, it strikes without warning, and it has a shattering effect because nobody is expecting it.

It was like that with Gary, one of our younger gunners. One moment he was a normal sailor going about his work in a normal way. The next moment he was a wild maniac, amok with a blade in his hands, bent upon murder.

Gary was a newcomer to our crew. He was assigned as a replacement one January day as we lay at anchor in New York Harbor, waiting for sailing orders.

He sat in my cabin while I went over his record. The

159

entries showed that, for a time, his service had been very good. Then it had turned bad. It was easy to understand the reason for this when you talked to Gary and when you understood what he had gone through.

He was seventeen years old, and had been an Armed Guard gunner for eight months. The ship he had served on during most of that time was an oil tanker that ran between New York and Caribbean ports. It was in the Caribbean Sea, while running alone and without escort, that Gary's tanker was spotted one night by a submarine.

One torpedo was all the U-boat needed. The ship exploded in a roaring eruption of flaming oil. Gary was blown clear of the inferno. He was hurled unconscious into the waves, and when the shock of the water brought him to his senses, he was floundering at the outer edge of a lake of writhing flames that spread between him and the sinking ship.

Two of his shipmates, his closest friends aboard, had been blown into the sea also. But not quite as far as Gary. They had landed just behind him in the blazing oil. And Gary had lived through the horrible experience of hearing their agonizing screams and watching helplessly as they died before his eyes.

Later that night, he managed to climb aboard a battered life raft and then he became unconscious again. When he came to his senses the next time, he was alone on the raft and the sun was rising in a hot blue sky; from horizon to horizon there was no sign of life. Three days later he was picked up by a passing ship and was put ashore at Key West. He spent the next month in a Navy Rehabilitation Camp.

When he was released, the doctors pronounced him fit.

He was sent back north to the Armed Guard Center at Brooklyn and immediately assigned to another ship. He promptly went AWOL, and his convoy sailed without him.

The Shore Patrol found him in upstate New York, and Gary drew a short term in the brig. Then he was assigned to still another gun crew, and again he went AWOL. He had just finished his second brig term when he reported aboard our ship, and he had scarcely had time to stow his gear below decks before he managed to talk his way onto a harbor launch and disappear once more.

In less than twenty-four hours, they picked him up in a southern Connecticut town and ticketed him for the brig once more. But I argued for him and got him returned to ship. I'm still not sure why I did it, except that Gary did not strike me as an incorrigible troublemaker, but rather as a scared kid who had been doing his best but who had not been given a fair chance to get over the terrible shock of seeing his shipmates burn to death. Repeated trips to the brig obviously were not going to help him but, perhaps, a voyage with a good crew might make him sound again. He was clean, intelligent, quiet, polite and, for the short time they had known him, he was well-liked by the other gunners. And so we took him along.

Things might have worked out if it had been a normal convoy voyage. But it got off to a bad start, and then it got worse.

We ran into trouble at the very beginning. At the New York convoy conference, on a Thursday afternoon, we were ordered to weigh anchor at 1:50 Friday morning. But at eleven o'clock that night, a thick wall of fog moved in from the open sea and locked New York Harbor in an impenetrable blanket that cut all visibility to zero.

We were sixty-five ships in all, and several did begin to move out on schedule, starting at one minute past midnight. By the time one hour had passed, it was a hopeless effort. The fog was so thick that some ships could not even find the channel opening in the harbor submarine nets, and they were groping around blindly in the lower bay, risking collisions with every turn of the screw. Many of the ships on hand, including ours, were heavily loaded with thousands of tons of high explosives. This meant that conditions were just about right for a major disaster.

Then at 1:45, as we were about to take in our anchor chain, we received a radio signal addressed to all ships in code: "Sailing cancelled. Masters and Navy officers report to Port Director's office at noon."

The fog was still thick and low on Friday when we went ashore for our revised orders, and were informed about various changes in the voyage plans. We also were informed that submarine contacts had been made during the night within five miles of the harbor entrance. Everything was clear now, though, they said. In any event, our orders were to sail at 3:50 Saturday morning—and we did.

Our first two days out, Saturday and Sunday, were more like springtime than midwinter. It seemed almost as though the fates were trying to make up for all the confusion of the immediate past hours. The sun shone bright and warm. The sea was calm and restful. Our lookouts stood watch in their shirtsleeves.

The North Atlantic, though, has a way of cracking down in an ugly mood just when life seems pleasant. In this case, the crackdown began with a wild storm that blew in on Sunday night. The wind rose and howled, the snow and rain lashed down, and before the night was over the ship was rolling so violently in the January gale that it was impossible for a man to stay in his bunk without holding a firm grip on the sideboards. Therefore, it was impossible to get much sleep.

Next day, the ordinary business of eating a meal became an intricate problem of how to use a fork with one hand, hold a plate steady with the other, and still find a way to fend off the rolling ketchup bottles and salt shakers. The sea had gone insane. By Monday noon, the convoy was scattered all over the horizon.

Then the storm subsided for a bit, just long enough for us to regroup and resume our course toward the coast of Newfoundland, where another forty ships were to join us for the eastward crossing. But before we got that far north, we lost a ship to the enemy.

It happened in dull daylight, about nine o'clock in the morning, when we were four days out of New York. The weather had turned bitterly cold, the sea was heavy with swells, and the sky had taken on the pale, thin light of a northern winter. We had been given no submarine warnings since leaving port, but apparently there was at least one U-boat trailing us and waiting for a chance to move in for a kill.

Then the chance came. An American Liberty, the leading ship in the tenth column, two columns to our port, suddenly went out of control, swung sharply to the left and plunged across the waves to smash heavily into an English freighter at the head of column nine. The collision ripped open a huge hole just forward of the bridge on the starboard side of the British ship. The gash ran from waterline to deck, and was as wide as a truck.

Both ships fell back out of convoy, but the damaged

Ninety-One was far worse off than the Liberty. She dropped back rapidly, and as we kept steaming ahead she was soon a full five miles astern of us, wallowing along all alone and barely making headway.

After a time, we watched a Canadian corvette detach herself from the escort screen and swing wide to start making her way back to the cripple.

Then came the first explosion with a brilliant burst of flame, a mushroom of smoke and steam, and a jarring eruption of sound waves that rushed across the water. Ninety-One had taken a direct hit.

The corvette promptly piled on speed and raced to get to her side. Before she could get there, Ninety-One took another hit. Two more explosions followed rapidly.

A plane hurried in from somewhere off to the west. It swung over the scene of action and roared low in tight circles a mile or so beyond Ninety-One's stern, spraying the waves with machine gun tracers. The corvette foamed to the spot and began dropping depth charges. Then the little warship opened up with her deck guns, and we saw a sudden flash of flame on the sea's surface.

After that, all was quiet. We had scored against the enemy. But Ninety-One was gone too.

Meanwhile, the Liberty regained her control and moved back into convoy position, with a jagged gash in her bow. For better or worse, she was going to try to make it all the way across.

That night, another storm roared in, even worse than the one that had lashed us earlier in the week.

From Thursday night to Tuesday, the wind howled and screamed, day and night. The waves turned black and ugly, and rose so high that they finally were looming above the bridge and smashing down on the boat deck.

We were drenched by rain and stung by sleet. The gunners had to cling to lifelines in order to fight their way to their gun positions without getting washed overboard. It was almost impossible to sleep, or even to sit and eat, without getting hurled to the deck.

That was one of the worst effects, the lack of sleep. By Tuesday everyone aboard ship was red-eyed, weary, and short-tempered. Every man was going through the same exhausting torture of being thrown from his bed, of trying to relax in a cabin chair only to have it tip as the ship rolled, of trying to escape the steep lurchings by walking around for a while only to be pitched from one bulkhead to another like a handball. It was even difficult to drink a cup of coffee without being thrown off balance and having it splash against your face or arms.

After a time, the convoy swung due south in a desperate effort to outflank the storm. But that meant moving into dangerous submarine waters, and before three hours had passed the familiar *WF* warning flags went aloft on the signal halyards of the Commodore ship, whipping out in the wind and the wet with their message of an enemy presence in the area. So then we had both the storm and the U-boats to contend with.

Through all of this, from the time of the New York fog, Gary had been doing his job well. He had stood his watches and rolled with the ship without grumbling. He had been unmoved by the collision of ships and the torpedoing of the British freighter. Because I was concerned about him, I had told a petty officer to watch him closely and to report to me if Gary showed any sign of strain. Now, with the storm and the submarine threat, I wanted to know how things were going.

"He's a good kid, Lieutenant," the petty officer said.

"He does his work and he gets along fine with the rest of the crew."

"Who does he get along with best?"

"Ames, I guess. They're on the three-inch gun together, on the same watch. And their bunks and lockers are alongside each other."

Ames was one of our best men. He was big, over six feet tall, and weighed 195 pounds. He had come to us from college football and had made four crossings with us. After his first crossing he had started a hobby, collecting foreign knives and bayonets.

"Tell Ames to let you know if Gary says or does anything peculiar," I said to the petty officer.

"I already did. The kid seems O.K."

That was just after the storm hit its peak and drove us south into submarine waters.

But now, with the ship still rolling in heavy seas, and with submarines somewhere nearby in the black of the night, Gary's quiet pressure-buildup had gone as far as it could without exploding. We didn't know it, but that's what had happened. The pressure was there, waiting for one little incident to touch it off.

It happened when Ames and Gary both came off watch at midnight. They struggled along the heaving deck and went below to the forecastle, where they shared bunk space with four other gunners. They were both drenched from the rain and the flying spray, and they peeled off their foul weather gear and started to towel themselves dry.

Ames was sitting on the edge of his bunk, removing his shoes, when the ship took a sharp, lurching roll to port that would have pitched him forward on his face if he hadn't reacted with speed. Instinctively, he straightened out his leg and slammed his foot against Gary's bunk to brace himself.

Gary froze for an instant, staring at him. Then he dropped his towel to the deck, crossed to where Ames was sitting, and glared down at his shipmate.

"Don't ever do that again," he said.

"Do what, Gary? I damned near went on my face, that's all."

"That isn't all," said Gary. "You put your foot on my bunk. I saw you do it. If you ever do it again, I'll cut off your leg."

Ames stared up at him in astonishment. He was ready to joke about it, but there was a tautness in Gary's voice and a sudden, strange wildness in his eyes that told him Gary was deadly serious.

"All right," Ames said quietly. "I'm sorry it happened. Now let's forget about it."

Gary shook his head. "No. I'll never forget it, and you mustn't either. Because if you do it again, I'll kill you."

"All right, Gary," Ames said. "I'll remember. Now let's drop it."

At that instant, the ship took another wild roll to port. Again Ames instinctively shot out with his foot, bracing himself against Gary's bunk.

Gary's face twisted in fury. Suddenly he screamed like an animal and went completely berserk. He leaped to Ames' locker, flung open the metal door, and grabbed an Italian bayonet. He swung around and hurled himself at Ames.

"I'll kill you! I'll kill you!"

Ames was startled, but he reacted instantly. He

warded off the bayonet thrust with one hand and knocked Gary back on his heels with the other. Gary leaped up and plunged in again, whipping the bayonet down at Ames' stomach. Ames twisted violently, dodged the blade, and landed a blow on Gary's chest that drove the crazed man backward. As he was about to charge in again, Gary was seized from behind by two other gunners who had come running at the sound of the fracas. They pinned his arms, wrenched the bayonet from his grasp, pushed him down on his bunk, and held him there. Then he collapsed in great shuddering sobs.

They brought him to my cabin and told me the story, and I told them to leave him alone with me for a while, that I wanted to talk to him privately.

He was over his sobbing by then, and he answered all of my questions in a quiet, polite voice. But there was no sense to what he said. He was too far gone to make sense.

"But why Ames?" I asked him. "All your shipmates get along with you, but Ames gets along with you best. You wouldn't really want to kill him, would you?"

"Yes—I'll try."

"Just because he put his foot on your bunk?"

"He's the only one who ever did that. That's why I'll kill him."

"Then you'll be tried for murder," I said. "Probably you'll be shot."

"I don't care. He shouldn't have put his foot on my bunk. I'll kill him."

"But he's been your good friend, Gary. He's helped you ever since you came aboard ship, hasn't he?"

"Oh yes, he's my good friend."

"And suppose you were sitting on your bunk and the ship rolled the other way. He wouldn't mind if you braced yourself against his bunk, would he?"

"No. He wouldn't mind."

"Then—"

"But I guess I'll kill him just the same."

After that, I did the only thing I could do with Gary. I set up a special guard watch, so that an armed man would be with him at all times for the rest of the crossing. His mind stayed twisted. He had lost all contact with reality. He was friendly with the other gunners when they spoke to him, but he seemed to have forgotten the names of all of them except Ames. He said several times that he would get around to killing Ames, but after a few days he seemed to have forgotten why.

When we got to England, I reported his case to the Navy authorities in London, with a full account of what he had gone through before joining our ship in New York. They agreed that what he needed was a term in a hospital, not a court-martial, and they arranged for him to be committed for treatment.

As they were removing him from ship, he came to my cabin under guard to shake hands and say good-bye.

"You've got a good crew, Lieutenant," he said, "and I'd like to join them, but the new orders you got for me have just come through and I've got to report right away."

"What new orders?" I asked. "Where are you reporting?"

"You know. I'm going on destroyers. That's where these men are taking me."

The guards shrugged helplessly and led him away, a mental babbler at an age when he should have been entering college or sitting in his home town drug store with some pretty girl.

Later in the day, Ames came to my cabin to ask if I had any idea why Gary, in his crackup, had turned against him rather than against one of the others.

"I keep trying," he said, "but I can't think of anything I ever said or did that might have hurt him. We never even had a mild argument. What do you suppose I did wrong, Lieutenant?"

"Nothing," I told him. "It could have been anybody. You just happened to be there when he broke up. And if you hadn't knocked him around, he'd have stabbed you."

Ames nodded. "And if he had stabbed me, I'd have bled cup custard. I was that scared."

On the return voyage, we had mental shakeups of a completely different sort. Instead of being grim and dangerous, they were relaxing and amusing.

They happened because our schedule went awry, and with it we lost our normal diet. Finally, we were down so low on our choice of food that all of us were getting mental vapors.

The trouble was that we were scheduled originally to sail directly back to New York from England, and so we followed the usual custom of giving away huge stocks of food to the British, keeping only enough on board to feed ourselves during the westward crossing. Unfortunately, after we had given so much away and were about to sail for home, our orders were changed at departure time. We were sent off on a lengthy side trip to the Mediterranean.

Thus instead of being back in New York in late February, we were still in the Mediterranean in April, living largely on what we could scrounge for ourselves in various ports, and that wasn't much. When we finally started back toward the States, our stores were down so low that even such staples as ketchup and canned milk were gone. (We had used the ketchup to make tomato soup.) Coffee and tea were low, jam had disappeared, the few eggs that were left were rotten, fresh fruit had vanished, our few remaining vegetables were browned and weary with old age. Three square meals a day consisted of two bowls of dry cereal and a cup of canned soup and, meanwhile, close to two weeks of sailing lay ahead of us before we could reach New York.

We discovered then that living on a diet of grapenuts does strange things to a man. The mind gets light and silly. Incidents that are normally ridiculous seem very serious, and the problems that are truly serious somehow seem cause for hilarity.

In the case of the First Mate, the diet of grapenuts produced an overpowering obsession with the doings of Tonto, the Lone Ranger's Indian pal.

The Mate lived for just one climax from day to day, which would come when he picked up the Lone Ranger's program on the ship's radio. He would listen avidly. To him, the Tonto story was the most important thing on the broadcast bands, far outranking any speech that might be made by Roosevelt or Churchill, and much more important than a daily news report on the course of the war.

And for hours at a time he would talk about what Tonto had done the day before, until finally his mood would change to one of anticipation as to what the brave Indian would be doing on the day following.

Eventually he got so he even talked like Tonto. It was not at all unusual to find him stalking the bridge, grunting to himself, and greeting his relief with: "Ho there, Kemo-sabi! We steady on course 255. I go below."

Life was like that all the way across to New York.

All good sailors like to look back in memory to the voyages they have made on a happy ship. We may have been the only ones in the Atlantic War ever to make a happy voyage on a silly ship.

CHAPTER SEVENTEEN

MEDICAL CHART

O UR INSTRUCTORS IN THE EARLY DAYS AT LITTLE Creek had warned us that, at some unexpected time, we might be called upon in an emergency to serve as ship's doctor. Sure enough, their forecasts proved accurate.

The standard gun crew equipment aboard a merchant ship came to include a medicine chest roughly the size of an old-fashioned steamer trunk. This occupied space in the gunnery officer's cabin, where it eventually seemed to take on a glowering, vindictive personality. Occasionally, when the ship rolled, the chest would charge at its keeper as though hoping to catch him off guard and break his legs.

The chest contained enough material to stock a small village pharmacy. It held large quantities of aspirin tablets, phenobarbitol pills, and laxatives. It held morphine syrettes and catgut sutures. It held splints, tourniquet bands, and instructions in how to tie off a severed artery. It held all manner of curatives including (as soon as they were available) the wonderful, new sulfa drugs. Probably the chest would have been a great help to a qualified doctor at sea, but the medical knowledge of the average gunnery officer usually did not extend much beyond the

173

cracker-barrel theory that a good treatment for bee-sting is a poultice of mud and ammonia. The prospect of having to use that knowledge in the middle of the ocean was thin at best.

To most of us, therefore, the chest was a hostile, depressing reminder of unwelcome responsibility made heavy by the weight of ignorance. But when there were 100 ships in convoy, with an average of sixty men aboard each ship, that meant that some 6,000 merchant seamen and Navy gunners had no doctor immediately available except the inexperienced officer in charge of the medical chest. Whether you could get a real doctor aboard in a case of harsh emergency would depend upon the right combination of conditions involving wind, rain, fog, high seas, hostile aircraft, submarine alarms, and the willingness of an escort ship to maneuver alongside and deliver a doctor on loan.

Most Armed Guard officers, therefore, prayed that they'd never be called upon to handle a medical crisis that couldn't be cured with aspirin tablets. Certainly the seamen and gunners must have been sending up the same sort of prayers nightly.

But things did happen. Accidents and sickness did develop, and when they did, they had to be treated.

One of my earliest patients on *Gulfwing* was an alcoholic merchant marine steward's mate who staggered aboard ship one midnight at departure time in New York, and who fell into his bunk unconscious. He woke up when we were about three hours at sea, and he found himself in the clutches of an acute case of delirium tremens.

Within seconds, he came howling down the passageway in a headlong flight of terror and pounded his fists on my cabin door.

"Lieutenant!" he screamed. "The worms and snakes are after me! They're crawling up my legs! Help!"

I heaved out of bed and flung open the door, and he leaped across my cabin and vaulted up onto a chair.

"Help me! They're all over the deck!"

I remembered reading somewhere that phenobarbitol tablets were supposed to quiet a person's nerves and, perhaps, put him to sleep, so I grabbed a bottle from the chest and dumped out a dozen or so of the pills and managed to cram them down his throat. Not knowing what to do next, I threw cold water in his face. That startled him so abruptly that he stared at me as though I were the crazy man, not he. But it stopped his screaming, and after a while he climbed down from his perch.

"Now get back to bed," I told him. "Those pills will put you to sleep in a few minutes. You'll be fine in the morning."

After he'd gone, I sat down with the instruction manual and did a little research about the effects of phenobarbitol and decided that, with the amount I'd given him, he might very well be dead by morning.

Fortunately, though, he came through in good shape. He was back at my door again the following day, shortly after breakfast, and I let him into my cabin and invited him to sit down.

"No, I've got to get to work," he said, fumbling with his cap. "I just wanted to stop by and thank you for helping me last night."

"You feel all right, then?" I asked.

"I feel fine, Lieutenant. Nothing's bothering me now except the bells."

"The bells?"

"Yes," he said. "The bells in my head. They've

been ringing ever since I swallowed all those pills."

That was not surprising. I watched him as he turned and went away, and I noticed that he kept punching himself on the head, just behind his right ear. Somewhere inside his skull, the bells must have been setting up a wild clamor. Next time, I thought, I would reduce the dosage a little.

A more serious case that came along one time was an acute attack of appendicitis. It never became bad enough for me to perform one of those classic wartime operations with bread knife, teaspoon, and sewing kit, but for a while I thought it might go that far.

The case developed on a westward crossing one late-August morning. We had just been through a one-day storm that had whipped the seas so high that for a time our bow was rising and falling thirty feet with the pitch of the ship. Then the storm had passed on in the night, and when the sun rose at four-thirty it rose on a clear, warm world but on seas that were still wild. We estimated that it would take us about ten days to reach New York, and we hoped that the summer sun would stay with us for that long. We were looking forward to a restful cruise.

At nine o'clock in the morning a sailor named Black, standing a forward lookout position on the 3-inch gun deck, suddenly let out a wailing scream, doubled over in agony, and fell unconscious.

When the alarm came over the battlephones, I hurried forward from the bridge and climbed the eight-foot ladder to the gun platform just in time to see him regain consciousness. It was too bad he did, for it brought him back to a world of pain. His right side, from cheek to toe, was paralyzed, and he seemed to be in shock.

I sent a runner to my cabin with the key to the medicine chest and told him to bring back all the morphine
syrettes. As soon as they arrived, we pulled down Black's
pants and stuck three of the syrette needles into his but-
tocks, one after the other, meanwhile swearing at them
for being so worthless that they wouldn't work. Then I
remembered that the needle tubes had to be punctured
before the morphine could flow.

Black was beginning to resemble a pin cushion by
then, but the fourth syrette needle seemed to take hold
properly. Even so, four of us had to hold him in his
writhings and lash him to a stretcher before the morphine
began to take effect.

As soon as he calmed down, we rigged up a pulley
arrangement to hoist his stretcher over the three-foot
shrapnel shield and lower it to the main deck. Then we
carried Black into the ship's hospital, the smoke-filled
paint locker. The usual marathon poker game was going
on there at the time, but the players agreed to give Black
a break and to move their game temporarily to other
quarters.

While all this was taking place, the ship's skipper
came down from the bridge to see what was causing the
excitement. He studied Black quietly for a few moments,
and then sadly shook his head.

"What's the matter?" I asked.

"I think he'll die," the skipper said. "He'll die unless
you operate, and if you operate, you'll kill him."

That sounded probable. Meanwhile, we raised flag
hoist *W* on a signal halyard, requesting immediate medical aid. The Convoy Commodore acknowledged our appeal by blinker light, and we flashed him an account of

the whole story. He in turn called the Escort Commander aboard a distant British destroyer, which apparently was carrying the only doctor in the convoy.

An hour later, we had the destroyer alongside, but the seas were still running high, too high to risk a ship-to-ship transfer of either the patient or the doctor. So we cruised along beam to beam at ten knots, in a shouted conversation involving reports of symptoms, temperature, pulse beat, diet, paralysis, age, weight, nausea, blood type, morphine dosage, allergy reactions, and instructions for treatment.

From then on, we had to keep somebody on watch with Black at all times. That made us short-handed, especially at night when the Commodore flashed submarine warning signals and when we had to man the guns and go into emergency turns. But short-handed or not, we had been told by the doctor to get hourly readings of pulse beat, which then ranged from fifty-two to eighty-four, and temperature, which swung from 96° to 103°.

I stopped in to visit Black in the middle of the night, and found he was able to talk in a thin whisper. I asked him if he wanted anything. He wanted to borrow rosary beads and a missal.

"And tell my father I was standing my watch," he said faintly.

"You're not going to die," I told him. But I wouldn't have taken bets on it.

The destroyer with the doctor aboard was back alongside early the next morning to receive our report on Black's condition and to give us further instructions for treatment. Apparently he did not like what we told him, for upon leaving us the destroyer sped off to the head of the convoy and closed in on the Commodore's ship.

We never knew what conversation passed between the doctor and the Commodore, but we discovered shortly that Black's case was changing the whole convoy operation. Right after the conversation with the destroyer, the Commodore's ship started running up a swift series of flag hoists that abruptly canceled all of our prearranged rendezvous positions and established new ones that lay along a direct line to New York. Our orders now were to bypass the northern-circle evasive route that we had been following and to take the shortest course for home.

As the last flag hoist came down, the convoy responded to signal and moved up to full speed ahead and off we went, steaming straight for New York Harbor.

Days later we made it, with Black still alive. But it wasn't easy. We had to roll through one more storm and then through thick fog. On the second night of the straight run, I was convinced we would lose our patient. That was when he took a sudden turn for the worse, and the gunner on watch at Black's bedside woke me up about three o'clock in the morning with an alarming report that the sick man's pulse was dropping rapidly.

I went below to the paint locker and checked the hourly chart and found that it read fifty-eight, fifty-four, fifty-two, forty-eight, forty-six. Half an hour later it was down to forty-two. Then it dropped to forty. At that point, not knowing what else to do, we opened a fifth of Scotch and woke up the patient and began pouring strong drinks down his throat.

Perhaps it was the worst possible treatment, but either it worked on its own or else we got the benefit of a remarkable coincidence. In any event, before long his heart seemed to pick up again, his pulse began to climb, and by the time daylight arrived it was pumping along at sixty beats a minute and Black was sleeping comfortably, if somewhat drunkenly.

With all the worry and trouble he had caused, Black nevertheless came through in the end as the most popular man aboard ship; he got us into New York two full days ahead of our scheduled arrival time.

The gunners showed their appreciation in their own way. With all of those extra liberty hours ahead of them, not a man left ship until the ambulance arrived to take Black to the hospital. Then they gave him a cheer as his stretcher passed by and they followed him ashore in a cluster. Some of them managed to hitch a ride to town in the ambulance cab.

Several weeks went by before I had any more serious cases to handle but then, on a crossing to Gibraltar, the work began to accumulate. Two men showed up at sick call with venereal disease infections, both of which were traced to a Boston tavern that ranked second only to the "Bunch of Grapes" in Suez on the official list of the world's worst VD sources.

Next came two gunners supporting a third one between them. He had run across the foredeck at night and collided with a taut steel cable, which took off a piece of his scalp. That meant giving him a head-shave and sprinkling him on top with sulfanilamide powder. Another gunner, Ames, complained of stabbing pains in his kidneys and thighs, but since I could find nothing in the book about treating such symptoms he had to settle for aspirin. Weeks later, his trouble turned out to be rheumatic fever, and we eventually left Ames in a London hospital.

Meanwhile, one of the merchant crew, a fireman named Jenska, had been coming in almost daily with complaints about chronic, severe headaches and spells of drowsiness. I had talked to Hartley, the ship's steward, about him, and together we had tried to figure out what was wrong and to treat him for it, but so far we'd had no luck. The headaches and the drowsiness continued.

Then, suddenly, Jenska complicated the puzzle for us by going into convulsions, frothing at the mouth, and winding up unconscious. Fortunately he was off watch and resting on his own bunk when the seizure hit him. We didn't know what to make of it.

We ran up flag hoist *W* and signaled to the Convoy Commodore for help, and in a matter of only a few minutes a destroyer, U.S.S. *McCormick,* had left her escort station and came foaming alongside. It was rough, dangerous work, for we were loaded with explosives, but the *McCormick* managed to rig a high-line connection between the ships, and over came a young Navy doctor.

We told him the story. He examined the fireman and asked a number of questions. Then he shrugged.

"I can't tell from here," he said. "Let's get him down to a mess table and we'll prop him up on the edge. Then each of you hold one of his shoulders steady and I'll tap his spine. But don't let him slip while I'm doing it, or the pain will drive him nuts."

It may have been a good idea, but not from Hartley's point of view. We stood braced on opposite sides of the patient, trying to hold him steady against the roll of the ship. The doctor tapped in, and nearly had his work done. But then the sight of a needle and tube sticking into Jenska's naked back proved too much for the steward. He turned white, abruptly dropped his end of the shoulder burden and reeled out to the passageway, violently sick to his stomach.

As Hartley let go, Jenska lurched sideways. The tube and needle jammed. He let out a wild shriek of pain. With that, the doctor called off the whole business, and together we got the fireman back to his bed.

There he answered everything the doctor wanted to know by having a full-scale epileptic seizure. Then he had four more in the next four hours.

This threatened to be a real problem, for we were still eight days from Gibraltar, and Jenska obviously was in bad shape. But, somehow, things worked out all right. The doctor left us a supply of strong dope pills, and advised a day-and-night watch over the fireman. Fortunately, the weather stayed fairly mild, and the *McCormick* was able to come alongside each morning to let the doctor make his high-line transfer, and then to leave him with us for a few hours while she went off scouting for submarines.

In the end, we made it safely to our destination, where we called upon British medical authorities and turned our problem over to them. By that time, our patient was probably the most heavily doped fireman in the merchant marine, and Hartley was the most confirmed anti-epilepsy steward.

As the voyages continued, so did the medical incidents. They took in ringworm, sunstroke, hernia, a man who crushed his thumb in a bulkhead door, a man who got his hand pulped under a falling hatch.

Once, aboard ship in Alexandria, I had to overcome the language barrier in order to fix up the mangled toes of an Arab stevedore whose foot had been caught under a falling cargo crate.

His friends brought him to my cabin, and he must have been convinced I was going to amputate, for he fought against them violently and howled and held back. There was genuine terror in his eyes. At last, they wrestled him into my quarters and then they left in a hurry, washing their hands of the whole business.

I locked the door so that the terrified Arab couldn't escape, and then I somehow got the message to him by gestures that I was going to make his foot better, not cut it off. After a while he sat down, holding himself rigid and wary, and allowed me to go to work.

His toes were in bad shape, but I did the best I could for them. Then I wrote out a pass permitting him to get hospital attention ashore. At that, his whole attitude changed. He seemed grateful almost to the point of hysteria. He prattled and sighed and rolled his eyes, and finally broke into a broad, happy grin.

I helped him out through the doorway, and watched him go limping back toward the main deck and then down to the gangway and ashore. I was feeling sorry for him, thinking that this was probably the first and last time in his miserable life that he'd ever have the benefit of sulfanilamide.

But when I got back to the cabin, my feelings changed. I discovered that while I had been kneeling down and fixing his toes, he had been busy reaching out in all directions and stealing things. He had walked off ship with two of my cigarette cartons.

I had mistaken his broad grin for gratitude.

At that, perhaps it was.

CHAPTER EIGHTEEN

THE SHADOW WAR

THERE WAS ONE IMPORTANT ASPECT OF CONVOY OPERA-
tions that was wholly overlooked in our early classes
at Little Creek. Nobody ever came forth to tell us how to
cope with the shadow war that went on just below the
surface of the official war. Nobody offered us any sugges-
tions about how to deal with espionage, sabotage, subver-
sion, or any other phase of the cloak-and-dagger world.

Perhaps that was because the Navy, in the early days
of the 1940's, did not expect us to encounter it; perhaps
because we, on our unglamorous and salt-stained ships,
were supposed to be remote from its touch.

But it did reach us, many times and in many different
forms. As the weeks turned to months, and then to new
calendar years, those of us from Little Creek who were
still on the convoy lanes would meet from time to time in
distant foreign ports and trade tales of our experiences
with furtive enemies whom we never saw. It struck us as
downright unsporting that they would single us out as
targets aboard our creaking Liberty ships and tankers,
but they did.

In their clandestine operations against us, they were
after two things. They were seeking information about
convoy routes and plans to be used in preparing hostile

submarine and aircraft attacks. And they were out to cripple a convoy ship, any convoy ship, whenever the opportunity arose, in order to weaken its defenses or force it to drop from formation and become a sitting target for torpedoes.

Looking back, it seems surprising that enemy agents did not enjoy far better success than they actually did in getting their hands on the convoy schedules. Certainly there were plenty of copies in circulation.

In New York, for example, if we were to sail to Britain in an 80-ship convoy, there would be 80 merchant skippers and 80 Armed Guard officers attending the convoy conference at South Ferry, plus the captains of perhaps sixteen escort ships. As we left, each of us would have in his briefcase or in his jacket pocket a mimeographed copy of the convoy plan.

This plan identified each ship by name and coded call letters, gave the ship's position in column formation, its tonnage, its cargo, its maximum speed, and its port of destination.

With all that information on hand, a submarine commander could know exactly how the convoy would look at sea, where it was going, when it was scheduled to arrive, and which ship would be singled out to make the biggest explosion en route.

More often than not, the merchant skipper and the Armed Guard officer would go straight from the convoy conference to the nearest tavern to talk over the upcoming voyage. Then, if there was still time before departure, each would go uptown for a farewell hotel rendezvous with his wife, which would mean a few more drinks and, if possible, a night on the town.

Looking back, it seems unbelievable that copies of convoy plans were not forever getting mislaid in the Cafe Rouge of the Hotel Pennsylvania or in the Hotel Dixie bus terminal.

Yet, that sort of thing rarely happened. And the one time that I know for certain it did happen, the enemy must have been looking the other way, for on that occasion we experienced no serious trouble.

That lone time that I know about took place late one sunny afternoon on lower Broadway, when a merchant skipper was so harried for time that he could not accompany his wife to her train at Grand Central Station but had to hail a taxi, hustle her inside, give her a quick parting kiss, and then grab another taxi for the dash to his ship. As it happened, he had placed his briefcase on the sidewalk during the kissing interlude, and he left it there, sailing plans and all, when he rushed off toward the docks.

We did not sail that night. Instead, we all received cancellation orders and had to report back for a second convoy conference the next day. There we learned that somebody had found the briefcase on the sidewalk and had turned it over to the Navy with all papers intact. But for all the Navy knew, those papers might have been copied and then replaced as subterfuge, which could mean that twenty or more submarines would be waiting for us at a place of their choosing.

All routes and convoy rendezvous positions had to be changed, therefore, and as a result we were forty-eight hours late clearing New York Harbor. We sailed without the briefcase skipper. We assumed, as we went out past Sandy Hook, that he was still sweating it out before a

Navy board of inquiry, trying to explain what had happened.

Sometimes, in New York, enemy agents would work the hotel rooms, looking for convoy plans that might have been left carelessly on a bureau top or in an open suitcase.

They came to visit my wife and me one evening in a midtown hotel. But we did not know about it until after they—or he—had left.

It happened on a spring night in the Easter season, when a big convoy for England was shaping up. Our conference was over and all plans were complete. We still had twenty-four hours before departure time, so three of us who would be sailing as Armed Guard commanders were spending our last night ashore with our wives, all under the same hotel roof. We had a pleasant party at the bar and a good dinner.

But while we had been wining and dining, somebody had been visiting our bedroom. Upon our return, we found that an eager intruder had searched through the contents of my suitcase. Fortunately I had not left my convoy papers where he could get them.

My wife's suitcase, too, had been ransacked. No jewelry or anything of value had been taken but, nevertheless, she had been robbed. For some unaccountable reason, our visitor had walked off with two big chocolate Easter eggs that she had bought that afternoon to take home to our children.

Whoever it was that had been in our bedroom obviously was no ordinary sneak thief. We discovered the following morning that he also had entered two other rooms on the same floor, ransacked the suitcases, and left without stealing any valuables. Those were the rooms of the two Armed Guard officers who were sailing with me in convoy that day, and who also had carefully hidden their papers where they would not be found.

We still wondered why the Easter eggs had been stolen. According to the police, this was done deliberately to mislead the military investigators.

Perhaps they were right. We couldn't argue with them, for none of us knew enough about the strange workings that go on in the mind of a spy. But I've always felt that perhaps our prowler just liked candy. Or maybe he had two children of his own, and discovering those eggs was a welcome, preholiday windfall.

Usually our contacts with espionage or sabotage attempts on shore amounted to little more than an interesting diversion. But at times, the enemy agents were with us at sea, and out there it was totally different. Out there, a successful enemy plot could mean death.

And they never stopped trying. On three different voyages—twice while carrying gasoline and once while carrying munitions—I sailed on ships where sabotage was attempted in midocean.

On one of those occasions, riding in an eastbound convoy on a black and starless night, we suddenly lost steering control and within seconds were plunging across-column and heading directly toward a ship on our starboard beam.

We made the switch to our emergency steering gear barely in time to ease off and avoid a collision that almost certainly would have blown up our ship and probably the other one as well. Later, when we investigated the source of the trouble, we discovered that somebody had used a hacksaw on a steel steering cable, cutting through all but two or three strands, which inevitably had snapped under strain.

On the other two occasions, the sabotage was in the engine room. Foreign matter had been dumped into the fuel supply lines, and the ship's huge diesels had floundered to a halt, leaving us to drift helplessly in mid-Atlantic while the convoy went along without us.

Each time that happened, though, the breakdown came on the morning of a clear, fair day, with the sea calm and with visibility sharp for miles around in all directions. Each time, we kept full manpower at the guns for a long space of hours, until the lines could be blown clear and we could feel the welcome rumble of the engines again and could move away at full speed to rejoin the convoy at the next rendezvous position. If submarines had been around (and we assumed they were), the combination of clear weather and the sight of our gun-readiness apparently had given them second thoughts, and they had stayed silent.

These incidents inevitably provided strong evidence that enemy operators had infiltrated the merchant crews and were with us twenty-four hours a day, looking for a chance to strike. They would have had to be fanatics, of course, for their lives were at stake as surely as were ours. But following each case, long days of investigation by United States intelligence officers in port failed to isolate any individual who could be blamed for the sabotage.

Over the long months, they struck at us in many ways, both directly and indirectly, and sometimes the ship was the target and at other times the target was our lives.

On one voyage, just after we had left London, a chance inspection of survival equipment disclosed that the batteries had been removed from all of the little red lights on our lifejackets. That could have meant abandonment and almost certain drowning for any man leaping into the sea at night. His lifejacket light was his best—and sometimes his only—means of attracting the attention of a rescue crew.

Another time, while in Liverpool, we had received orders assigning us to a high-risk mission in the Mediterranean, and we were told to draw several thousand extra rounds of 20-millimeter ammunition before leaving port. But when we spot-checked and tested that ammunition at sea, we found it was worthless. Sabotage on the inside of some factory in England had altered the shell casings just enough to prevent them from fitting into the guns.

But probably the most direct blow that was thrown at us by the hostile shadow people came during a wild night when we were bound east for Africa and had run into an autumn gale.

We were six days out and in submarine waters when, at about half an hour after midnight, the lookout-gunners on my six-man watch section suddenly began toppling like trees in a hurricane.

The night was a torrent of rain at the time, and the wind and the sea were raging. I was on the bridge with the skipper when an alarmed report came in over the battlephones from the 5-inch gun at the stern. One of the gunners back there had been stricken with violent stomach pains.

I hurried back, struggling through the wash of waves across the deck, and found the man writhing about on the gun platform, clawing at his abdomen and gasping with pain.

He was a heavy six-footer, and he couldn't even stand, let alone walk. That meant he would have to be carried if we were going to get him to shelter.

Two petty officers, summoned from a card game below decks, fought their way through the storm and arrived with a stretcher, and somehow we transported the gunner through the drenching darkness with the ship rolling almost on her beam. We got him back to his quarters amidships, and there we undressed him and got him into bed.

This, I supposed, was a duplicate of Black's attack of appendicitis, so I injected the patient with a morphine syrette to ease his pain.

But it was not appendicitis. It was poison of some kind. That became clear in a matter of seconds, when another emergency call came from the 3-inch gun forward. Both men there had been stricken in the same way, so badly that one of them could only scream in pain while the other struggled to gasp his cry for help into the battlephones.

With that, I rang General Quarters and turned out the whole crew. In the short time it took the gunners to rush to their stations, all remaining men on the watch detail had been struck down and were writhing and twisting and groaning in their agonies. They lay there at their guns, helpless in the storm, retching and vomiting and tearing at their throats and stomachs.

From there on, we had a wild three hours, a nightmare of fighting the gale, carrying the patients below, administering emetics, emptying their stomachs, trying to keep balanced on a heaving deck, and slipping on vomit.

In the midst of all this chaos, we heard the whistle on the Commodore's ship sending the convoy into two sharp emergency turns and blasting a submarine-attack alarm, but fortunately whatever action there was that night took place on the far side of the columns and never involved us with our undermanned guns.

By three o'clock in the morning, we had the crisis well in hand. The sick gunners by then were weak and shaky, but they were apparently out of danger and on their way to recovery.

By four o'clock, two of them were back on their feet, still unsteady but able to talk rationally. They agreed upon one thing, that they never had suffered such pain in their lives.

It was obvious what had been done. An attempt had been made to put an entire watch section out of action, all at once and at a time when submarines were about to close in.

But how it was done, we never did learn. My two petty officers and I probed the case as far as we possibly could. We questioned every man in the gun crew and every man in the merchant crew, looking for some kind of a lead. But it was hopeless; it remained baffling.

It boiled down to the fact that the six men had eaten dinner together that night, but some had eaten one thing and some another. The only thing that all six of them had shared was tea.

But other men, both Navy gunners and merchant seamen, had also had some of the same tea, and some of the same food as well, without experiencing anything unusual whatever.

Somehow, therefore, the six men slated to go on watch at midnight, with stormy seas and submarines to contend with, had been singled out and had been poisoned; and nobody else aboard ship had been touched. None of us

ever could figure out how the poison had been adminis-
tered so selectively.

It remains a mystery to this day.

Later, there was the mystery of the silent radio, but
that one we managed to solve. It was not sabotage; it
was incredible stupidity.

It happened in late 1943, when the merchant marine
was training and sending to sea its own batches of wartime
radio operators, to replace the Navy operators who by
then were badly needed aboard ships in the Pacific fleet.

We drew two of the new graduates, fresh from their
radio-school classrooms in Boston. On their first day
aboard, when we were two hours out at sea on a voyage
to Bristol, they came running to my quarters with an
alarming report. Somebody must have been tampering
with the equipment in the radio shack, they said. They
couldn't get a thing to work; nothing was going out and
nothing was coming in.

For the next four days, we were the most embarrassed
ship on the Atlantic. We knew by our communications
schedule exactly when certain messages should be coming
in for us, but all we could do about it was to use the
blinker light and the flag hoists to ask the ships around
us to let us know what was going on. They answered our
questions, but they did so with the gentle, direct approach
they might have used toward retarded children.

Meanwhile, the two radio men from Boston kept tink-
ering with their equipment, sending out calls that never
went anywhere and sitting at their instruments for hours,
straining for messages that never arrived. At one point,
out of desperation, we blinked to an escort ship to come
alongside, and we told her our troubles. For an hour or

more she foamed right along on our beam, transmitting directly to us from only fifty yards away, and still we couldn't receive her messages.

Finally on the fifth day, one of my gunners came to me on the bridge and asked permission to look over the dead radio equipment and talk to the bewildered operators.

"I run my own ham radio station out in Iowa, Lieutenant," he said. "Maybe I can help those guys."

"If you're that good, why aren't you in communications?" I asked him.

"I'd rather shoot guns."

"Go ahead down there," I told him.

And he did.

He walked down to the radio shack, stood in the doorway, and looked around the room.

"Having trouble?" he said to the operators.

"That's it. Trouble."

"First let's check your circuit loads."

"Our what?"

"And your main power switch, your circuit switches, your fuse capacity."

"Sure."

The gunner stepped inside, pulled things here and there, twisted a few dials, replaced a fuse, and then without a word walked out and went back to his lookout post.

Less than ten minutes later, one of the operators approached the bridge very sheepishly, and handed me the first radio message we had received since leaving port.

Ironically, it was an order to all ships to maintain radio silence.

CHAPTER NINETEEN

ACTION BELOW

THE SCOREKEEPERS WHO EVENTUALLY WROTE THE
official records of World War II have counted our
merchant marine losses in that conflict at 5,579 men
among the dead and missing, 487 taken prisoner, and 984
ships sunk. Most of those 984 ships were destroyed by
enemy submarines, and on most of them, the Navy gunners were the last men left aboard. They had known that
might be their lot when they volunteered.

The most desperate and costly battles, of course, were
fought in the war's early days, when the U-boats struck
and scored almost as they pleased, and when death and
destruction overhung the convoys like evil clouds.

Those first gun crews to go out from Little Creek went
to sea at a time when the submarines were sinking better
than one ship a day in the Atlantic. By March, 1942, the
sinkings were up to more than two ships a day, with oily
debris and charred bodies washing ashore along the Atlantic Coast from Maine to Florida. The flames of burning tankers could be seen from the beaches at night.

Between those terrible hours and the D-Day zero hour
of June 6, 1944, a daily average of 5.4 Armed Guard gun
crews reported aboard American merchant ships to help
fight a path through the ranks of enemy raiders and to

deliver overseas the millions of tons of war supplies necessary for final victory. If they had not won through, the
decisive invasions of Europe could not have been made.

They won their private war; but it was never easy.

Even as late as 1944, the Germans came up with a
number of new weapons to help them block the Atlantic
convoys, and the men from Little Creek suddenly found
themselves fighting against such strange instruments as
magnetic torpedoes and sonic torpedoes, designed to home
in on a ship no matter what sort of evasive tactics were
used. Also, the Germans that year developed such power-
ful new submarines that in one instance, in a fight in the
Caribbean Sea, a lone U-boat fought back for ten hours
against six Navy planes, a Navy blimp, and an Army
bomber before it was sunk.

Nevertheless, in the spring of 1943, the tide began to
swing so disastrously against the submarines that the convoys from then on outkilled their enemies at an astonishing
rate. And as the rate climbed, the once-glamorous German submarine service eventually became so wracked
with fear and mutiny that the Berlin government had to
draft crews and force them to sea to man the big U-boat
fleet.

Still they fought on, sometimes with the help of Japanese submarines that cruised from halfway around the
world to help their Axis partners in the Atlantic—and in
some cases, to be destroyed there. Finally, even within
scant weeks of the end of the European war, they tried
a last-chance assault with a fleet of new supersubmarines
that headed westward across the Atlantic, intent on getting within range of the United States East Coast. Most
of that fleet went down to destruction under attack in

midocean, a few of them got through to coastal waters and torpedoed five merchant ships, and the last of the lot was sunk between Block Island and Newport Harbor barely two weeks before VE-Day.

Meanwhile, though, we encountered a stubborn sort of courage among some of Admiral Doenitz' U-boat commanders that was both admirable and foolhardy, and that made it always dangerous to relax on convoy duty, no matter how peaceful the surrounding conditions might appear.

We tangled with one of that brave and desperate breed on a warm summer day in 1943, at a time and a place when the last thing in the world we had expected to meet was a fighting U-boat.

It was on a Sunday morning, when we had just completed an Atlantic crossing from New York to the waters of Northern Ireland. Our convoy of sixty ships had changed from its ocean-going formation of nine columns to a long, two-file formation, and we were sailing down through the North Channel, with Ireland's Benmore Head close at hand to starboard and Scotland's picturesque Mull of Kintyre looming softly in the distance to port.

It was an ideal time for relaxing. The midmorning sun was clear and warm, and the channel sea was flat. The Irish shore lay calm and beautiful, as though enjoying a welcome Sunday rest.

We were feeling safe and secure for the first time in two weeks, knowing that the mid-Atlantic attacks were temporarily behind us and that the wolfpacks were many miles astern for now. As we cruised along, we on *Gulfwing* were near the head of the inshore column, and some of the gunners were sunbathing on the foredeck while others were listening to a merchant seaman playing sad songs on his harmonica. The usual six lookouts were at the guns, stripped to their shorts, soaking up the sun's rays, and watching over a sea's surface that was smooth and placid and shone like soft blue silk.

We rounded a promontory that sheltered a wide bay off to the right, and we straightened out and followed in line of wake for the journey across the bay's broad mouth.

Then, without warning, we were under attack.

The violent bang of a deck gun shattered the Sunday calm. A screaming shell ripped the air not twenty feet over our heads and plunged into the sea off the port side of the ship hurling a brilliant geyser into the sky.

The gunners almost outran the sound of the alarm gong in getting to their posts. As they manned their weapons, we came under fire again from a second shell, and through the glasses we could see a surfaced U-boat, lying well within the harbor. Her gunners already were slamming home a third round to hurl directly at us, probably because we happened to be the first tanker to show in her sights.

The action was over within seconds after it began. As the first shell exploded, a destroyer in the escort line to starboard fired two white rockets into the sky to alert the ships astern. Then she spun around in a foaming wave and tore down upon the U-boat, blasting away with 20-millimeter shells and with her 3-inch deck gun. At the same time, an RAF plane roared down the length of the convoy columns, rocking its wings in the alarm signal, and then banked sharply to the right to swoop down on the submarine with machine gun fire and bombs.

The U-boat never did get to fire her third shot. She

went down in the flaming attack, ripped and broken. In a matter of minutes all that was left to show she had ever existed was a widening patch of oily debris, floating on the calm North Channel surface.

It had been a strange and suicidal attack. The submarine commander certainly must have known, when he took up his ambush position, that there was no way he could hope to escape destruction.

By going into the shelter of the bay, he had deliberately placed himself in a spot from which he could not flee. By lying in wait for us there, hoping to surprise us as we rounded the promontory, he had cut himself off from all access to the open sea. Under the bright, warm light of the midmorning sun, he must have known he would be spotted on the surface the instant he got off his first round.

And why the deck gun at all? The only answer could be that he had expended all of his torpedoes in action somewhere under the ocean, and rather than return directly to home port for a fresh supply, he had chosen to slip into unfriendly waters and wait there for one last, hopeless crack at his enemy, even though it would cost him his life and his ship.

It was an act of almost incredible daring and of utter, unfathomable futility. Still, if he had ranged his first shot twenty-five feet lower, he would have sent one tanker down in flames.

At the time, it seemed a strange case for the records. But as it turned out, with the tide of warfare beginning to run against them, others of Doenitz' submarine commanders began to take similar individual actions against impossible odds.

Once, for example, when we were anchored off Perth in the Firth of Tay, the word was quietly passed by Aldis lamp, flashing from ship to ship, that a U-boat had been detected entering the anchorage waters, and then had been lost to contact. There were forty of us in there at the time, all heavily laden with munitions for London, all waiting through a dim and misty twilight for the arrival of darkness, when we would weigh anchor and head out for the voyage down the channel. And now, somewhere among the broadly-spread forty hulls, there was a lone submarine searching for a target.

We knew that he dared not show his periscope, that the best he could do would be to grope around under the murky waters, trusting to luck and to electronics to line up something for his torpedoes. To confuse the submarine still further, all of us on signal started our propellors churning, and we sat there with our anchor hooks down, stirring up a vast sea of roiling mud, while our heavy grinding screws and rolling blades rotated in a way that was certain to make utterly worthless any undersea detector devices. We kept that up through the dusk, while destroyers and patrol boats prowled slowly back and forth through the lines of anchored ships until, finally, the jarring thump of depth charges sent shuddering waves across the harbor, and we knew that the lurking enemy had been located and destroyed.

By then it was dark and time to depart, so we kept our propellors churning while, one by one, we pulled in our creaking anchor chains and moved slowly out of the firth and started down the southbound convoy channel. The incident was over.

Later in the year, another daring U-boat commander

moved in against us as we lay moored in the harbor at Alexandria. He came in shortly after sundown and was detected by surface patrol craft almost at once, then was lost to them. But we knew he was out there somewhere in the harbor, hiding from the British planes that flew low across the surface in search of him, and eluding the destroyers that curved back and forth, trying to establish contact.

He was still there several hours later, when the hunt was called off. But like his colleague in the North Channel incident, he must have exhausted his supply of torpedoes, for he chose a unique method of attack. He used frogmen.

They approached our ship shortly after midnight, apparently intent upon fastening demolition charges to our hull and our propellor blades.

It was only by chance that we spotted them. Two Navy gunners with nothing else to do had gone up to the 5-inch gun deck at the stern, to while away their time with a third gunner who was standing watch at that position. It was a hot night, and the harbor surface was a dark, flat, oily calm. After a while one of the idle gunners moved to the stern rail where he leaned far over and stood there bracing on his elbows, staring down at the black water and amusing himself by spitting at his own reflection.

He could not possibly have been in a better place at a better time, for suddenly where his reflection had been so calm and quiet, he saw bubbles rising and water rippling. To his astonishment, two frogmen were swimming into view at a spot right under his eyes, and they immediately went to work on the ship's propellor.

He did exactly the right thing. He did not ring the

General Quarters alarm, which would have frightened the swimmers away with its clang and clatter. He did not say a word about his discovery, even to his two shipmates. Instead, he turned away quietly and went below to get the 30-caliber rifle that the gun crew kept handy for shooting at enemy mines. Then he returned to the stern of the ship and found that the angle of fire was too sharp to allow getting off a good shot. So he went ashore with his rifle, took up a position on the dockside nearby, and fired ten steel-jacketed shells into the bubbling water.

We never did know whether he killed or wounded anyone. All we ever knew was that the frogmen were gone in a matter of seconds, either escaping together or with one dragging the other one after him. About an hour later, we received an alert from the Royal Navy headquarters on shore, reporting that a submarine had been detected slipping out of the harbor at fast speed, and to be on the watch for any others that might be around.

The next morning, shortly after daylight, we had a Navy diver go down to look the ship over underwater and examine her hull, from nose to stern.

He found one demolition package with German markings, lying down there in the mud, just under the propellor shaft.

CHAPTER TWENTY

ACTION ABOVE

FROM THE MUD BELOW TO THE SKY ABOVE, AND FROM horizon to horizon, was the changing arena in which the men from Little Creek fought against the enemy in order to deliver war supplies overseas.

And although submarines admittedly were the big enemy, it was in the sky overhead that some of the hardest battles of the convoy ships were fought. The worst of these were fought above the docks of London, between Navy gun crews aboard ships moored in the Thames and the last desperate fliers of Hermann Goering's angry *Luftwaffe*.

It was an ugly, brutal, no-holds-barred battle, and it raged for close to two weeks in the days and nights of February, 1944. They called it "The Second Blitz," "The Baby Blitz," "The Battle of London," and "London's Last Stand," depending upon whether you were reading the newspapers of Liverpool, Manchester, London, or Berlin.

By that time, many of the Armed Guard veterans were experienced performers at fighting off air attacks. We had fought the German planes on the Mediterranean run, when they crisscrossed from southern Europe to Africa. We had fought them on the Murmansk run, when they roared out heading north from their bases in Norway. We

203

had battled them in the English Channel, where they attacked from Holland and Belgium. We had met them head-on, when they swooped in low over the Bristol Channel and the hills of Swansea. We had come to expect them at the entrance to the North Channel on the upper coast of Ireland, when they would come diving down for a last assault on the ships that had beaten off the submarines in midocean. We had fought them from the high-cliff confines of Scottish lochs and from the bleak surface of the North Sea and from their own front yard on the Bay of Biscay. We had met their first robot bombs in the Mediterranean, their Stuka dive bombers off the shores of Italy, and their Dorniers off Denmark. Since we had generally come out on the winning side, we felt there was nothing new or startling that they could show us.

But we had a lot to learn. We had never been through the hurricane fires and the nightmarish fury of a London blitz. And neither we nor anybody else in the world had ever faced anything like Hitler's V-1 and V-2 rockets that were then being readied in Europe.

The second London blitz could have been foreseen, if we had taken time to think about it. It was almost inevitably certain to take place.

By February of 1944, the Germans knew as well as we did that all of England was one huge munitions dump. They knew the countryside was crowded with incredibly strong and eager armies that were ready at a signal to storm the European continent with an assault power unequalled in history. The only way to hit this striking force, and to gamble on paralyzing it, was through the air.

With that in mind, Marshal Goering brought together all the bombing planes he could safely accumulate from

Germany's far-flung lines of action. He spent weeks putting them in top condition and preparing them for an all-or-nothing assault. Then he unleashed them, and he struck England with the mightiest blow the nation had been dealt since the original Battle of Britain in September, 1940.

The first week of the aerial onslaught had barely got under way when our ship turned in from the Channel and poked slowly up the Thames Estuary. We tied up at the Royal Albert Docks again, with 8,000 tons of munitions.

That was on a murky, rain-soaked Friday night in February. Just after midnight, when Saturday was only twenty-five minutes old, a petty officer woke me up in my bunk.

"Listen to that," he said. "We've got trouble."

I put my ear to the porthole, and faint and far away I could hear the wail of sirens moving steadily closer as the alarm kept pace with the planes coming across from France and roaring up the river toward us.

Our general orders, in all ports of call, were to remain dark and quiet under air raid conditions, and never to fire our guns unless we were directly singled out for attack by the enemy. This, we had been told, might enable us to survive an area air assault without being discovered and without risking our cargo.

But with thousands of tons of explosives on board, we knew that if the moment of personal attack arrived, it would be too late for defensive action. That could mean swift and bloody death for all hands. All it would need was one direct hit.

Rather than risk a disaster like that, most of us in the convoy ships preferred to ignore the orders and to fight back at the first opportunity. At the Royal Albert Docks, that was the only sensible thing to do, for we were tied up squarely in the middle of a prime target area. Nearby on shore, across the open flats, stood the Woolwich Arsenal. Just down the stream from us, and across the water, a huge British aircraft carrier rested in drydock, propped up in a helpless position atop braces and girders. Just off our beam lay acres of "Operation Mulberry" equipment, the broad floating docks that Winston Churchill had invented to be towed to the French coast and interlocked there in order to create artificial invasion harbors. In such a vulnerable position, we had as much chance of going undiscovered through an air raid on that particular area as a bat would have had on the bullseye of a rifle range.

As the siren wails came closer, we manned our guns. We had to do it with only half a crew, for the rest of the gunners were enjoying shore liberty that night and were sampling life among the Soho pubs.

The roar of London's antiaircraft fire came steadily and swiftly up the river, accompanied by a rolling barrage of searchlight glares. Then the first attacking wave was directly overhead, in a melee of throbbing engines and blinding streaks of light. The din was incredible. Guns hammered away on all sides. Rocket launchers screeched. Bombs came thundering down. Incendiaries screamed and sparkled and touched off great fires. Chandelier flares lit up the sky with their weird and ghastly orbs. Shrapnel banged and clattered on the dockside and on the decks of our ship.

We pumped away at our guns as the first wave roared on toward the heart of the city. Within moments a huge red glow brightened the sky in that direction and the glare of it spread like a growing mushroom. The sound of racing fire engines could be heard in the midst of all the racket, and somehow it was a sound that seemed friendly and reassuring.

Then the second wave came pounding in, and swung off to the right to attack the Woolwich Arsenal. Great sheets of flame flashed up as the bombs struck home and burst.

The third wave tore straight overhead, then swung sharply to the left and began to hammer the Mulberry Docks and the aircraft carrier. That left our ship directly in the middle of a huge, brilliant, deafening triangle, with concentrated attacks going on at each corner. Bombers and interceptors kept crisscrossing above us, racing from angle to angle. The arsenal, at one point, took a straight twenty-minute pounding before the planes over its roof were driven away. The flames in the heart of the city spread and multiplied until at one moment, from the bridge of our ship, we counted sixteen conflagrations, without counting the minor one-building fires. Directly at dockside, close to our ship, squads of London's firefighters worked doggedly and daringly to smother the falling incendiaries that might at any moment have sent us all up in flaming destruction on a multithousand-ton burst of high explosives.

The show went on for one hour and ten minutes before the last of the enemy planes could be heard heading back toward its base on the continent. Then the All Clear sounded, and the guns were put back to bed.

Next morning, the British press reported that: ". . . an attempt was made to reach the heart of London. Gunfire was heard in several areas. An unidentified aircraft was detected passing overhead but was driven away."

Those raids became a nightly event, sometimes preceded by daylight attacks, for this was the *Luftwaffe's* last desperate show of strength, and failure here would mean inevitable failure to win the final victory. Therefore, nothing was spared. Everything that could be put aloft from a German base was sent over on attack.

As the nights went on, we grew accustomed to having fires all around us. We got used to having piles of hot flak littering our decks. We kept a mounting score of planes that we claimed to have shot down, though we knew we never would be able to prove our figures in view of the hits scored by "London's heaviest barrage of the war." The conservative British press finally began to give recognition to our efforts and to the efforts of several million others:

"Thirteen Nazi raiders were brought down last night," said the story on the fifth day. "This is the best score over Britain since the new series of raids began. The score is likely to be increased, for other claims are being investigated. From the outskirts of London, it seemed as though the raiders were showing a more healthy respect for the barrage than on the previous night.

"An extraordinary large number of flares drifted across London in great constellations, turning night into day. Fire guards in one area counted more than fifty in one small section of sky.

"Our rocket guns sent up clusters of flaming red balls. After hanging in the sky for a second, making a display as picturesque as a Crystal Palace fireworks night, the balls went off with a series of explosions and vivid flashes."

As an American newspaperman, I winced at that

story, and at the general coverage being given by the
London papers. The radio reports of the German News
Agency were much closer to our familiar style:

"Twelve thousand buildings have been destroyed in the
new phase of the Battle of London and another 60,000
have been damaged. One German plane is missing."

The London press, however, came through a day or
so later with an attempt to show what was going on in the
field of human interest. The papers carried photographs
of Churchill plodding across acres of smoking ruins, and
cracking: "Just like old times."

Night after night after night, the raids went on, working up toward a climax when hundreds of planes overhead
were being brought under fire by thousands of guns, all
roaring away at once. Nightly the black tidal water of the
Thames became a shimmering carpet of brilliant red
reflections; the sky became a blazing montage of rockets
and flares and flaming planes and sweeping searchlights;
the waters around us splashed and hissed under a rain of
falling hot steel; the huge ships that were moored at dockside literally shivered and shuddered under the shock
waves in the air and the vibrating waters of the big river.

Then, finally, the Germans called it off. There came a
night when we waited for them, but they did not arrive.
They had failed, they knew it, and they were through.

They left a memory of black walls silhouetted against
red glares, of helmeted firemen balancing atop tall ladders,
of brilliant rocket gun barrages skipping across the night
sky, of searchlights pinpointing a bomber against the
clouds while the guns from below brought it tumbling
down like a twisting meteor, of bodies in the streets and
walls crashing down, of weeping families and lost homes,

of gun-recoil jarring the ship's deck, of the whole Thames area turning red with fire glare and the whole sky turning white.

But whatever they had set out to achieve, they had lost. London was still in the fight, and had only to clean up its fire-blackened areas to get on with the job at hand.

It was the last time in the long and miserable war that the Germans showed up in aerial strength, and in person, over London's chimney tops.

But they had not yet struck their last blow. They still had two more tactical assaults to launch, one with the V-1 flying bombs and another with the V-2 rockets.

Many of us who were still in the Armed Guard were on hand for both of those assaults, for when the "V" weapons were introduced we were still hauling supplies across the ocean and either tying up to leave them at the Thames docks or, later, putting them ashore in France.

The V-1 "buzz bombs" became familiar and unwelcome acquaintances. Sitting on the Thames tide, we could spot them coming in from across the channel, coming up the river from Margate and Southend, racing in above the heart of the city with their exhaust flames glaring against the night sky and their engines humming like high-speed motor boats on Long Island Sound.

They were easy to hit, for they held a level altitude and they followed a straight course, until the abrupt cutoff of their engines brought them diving down to spread fire and death. But to hit them was one thing, and to destroy them was quite something else. On many a night, we hammered them with 20-millimeter shells, watching the tracers strike home and bounce off their sides; we learned that the only way to blow them up in midflight was to connect with a lucky hit squarely on the warhead, and that rarely happened. The only way to escape them was to listen for the cutoff of their engines and then, if the silence came directly overhead, dive desperately for the nearest shelter.

Life with the V-2 rockets, however, was considerably different. They were cold and detached and we never quite got to know them because they would arrive without warning. If a street or a building or a ship suddenly exploded before our eyes, we knew that another V-2 had reached London, and the rushing sound of its arrival would come along a few moments later to confirm this. The V-2 assault was our first and only experience with the world of supersonic weapons, and we had no way whatever of coping with it. Fortunately, the launching pads in Europe were wiped out before the V-2 could achieve the terrible destructive toll for which it was designed, and of which it was fully capable.

And for some of us, in a homebound convoy heading up the Channel, our last glimpse of a V-1 flying bomb was something that will always make us wonder if, perhaps, the Germans didn't eventually regret ever having invented the thing.

We were cruising north past Great Yarmouth on a black night when that final "buzz bomb" came roaring out from France, heading blindly for some unsuspecting, inland English town.

We watched it flaring against the night sky, its engine throbbing, its exhaust flaming like the tail of a red comet. We lined it up in our gunsights, ready to hammer it when it came within range.

But, then, as smoothly as though steered by hand, it

swung into a sharp curve that completely reversed its course. The last we saw of it, it was racing back toward some point on the Continent where its engine inevitably would go into its deadly stall, and it would dive down through the black sky to attack its masters.

We gave it a silent cheer, and then went back to worrying about mines and submarines.

CHAPTER TWENTY-ONE

THE RISING CREST

W<small>E SAILED NORTHWARD UP THE IRISH SEA LATE ON</small>
a midspring day in 1944, and somehow we sensed
that the final act of the convoy saga was now taking
shape. There was something about the start of that home-
ward voyage that had been missing from the other westward crossings. There was a feeling of impending change,
a growing awareness that the time had almost arrived
when the war would move on without us.

We did not know at the moment that more than a full
year lay ahead before the guns would fall quiet on the
Continent. But we did know then, even before any cross-
channel invasion had begun, that the war was about to
move inland from the Atlantic, and that the inevitable
outcome would be the defeat of Germany. We knew because we had carried the cargoes that would make that
defeat certain, and because we had taken them into every
corner of Britain. In doing so, we had seen the colossal
buildup that had taken place.

All over the land, the invasion forces were primed and
ready to move. Once they were unleashed, we knew that
nothing could hold them back or stand long in their path.

North in the lochs of Scotland, hidden behind story-
book hills with their gaunt castles and their misty peaks,

we had seen the crouching, gray units of an enormous naval assemblage. Up there in the quiet waters, waiting in the mist, we had seen aircraft carriers and cruisers, battleships and destroyers, submarines and landing barges, huge luxury liners that had been converted into great troop transports, scores of tankers and freighters swinging heavily at their anchor chains.

South on the fields of England, we had seen the en-campments of massive bodies of troops. In the railroad stations of London and Liverpool, we had watched thou-sands of combat-loaded soldiers file aboard the trains that would take them to the southern coastal ports. On the highways across the English countryside, we had seen mile upon mile of trucks and tanks and jeeps and mobile artillery drawn up along the roadsides. On many of our trips ashore, we had seen an incredible number of all types of warplanes, scattered from airbase to airbase, waiting.

We had felt a tension in the country that we had never felt before, a feeling of excitement and suspense among the people, like the taut anticipation that grips a mam-moth football stadium crowd on the day of the big game, just before the kickoff whistle blows.

There was no longer any question about it. The inva-sion across the Channel was coming soon. The armies and the navies were ready, and now were merely waiting, waiting, waiting.

We felt that the war with Germany would soon be moving on, passing beyond our reach. We wondered where we would go next, what we would do when the convoys were gone.

The Irish Sea, on that day of westward departure, was in a soft and quiet mood. It was a caressing sea, gentle with our ships. It was as smooth as a valley pond, clear and unrippled except for the whispering wash of our wake.

There were ten of us in line, stretched out in a straight column, cruising north at a restful six knots, with one British destroyer in the lead and another at the column's end. We were to join fifty other ships on the next day, convoy sections from Belfast, Aultbea, and Oban, before moving into voyage formation for the Atlantic crossing. Meanwhile, there were just the ten of us with our two destroyers, lazing up the Irish Sea under a setting sun, watching the changing colors of the coast of England far off to the right.

Then twilight came down, and it brought with it one of those rare, unforgettable hours when the whole world seems to stop for a quiet rest and to hang suspended in time, when the air is hushed and motionless and the sky and the sea are calm, when the smallest sound seems to travel with the clarity of a tinkling silver bell across mile after mile of water.

We sailed on through the twilight stillness, in a hush so complete that a single soft-spoken word on the deck of the ship ahead of us came floating back as clearly as though it belonged on our ship instead.

And then, in that perfect quiet, a sailor on the British destroyer far out ahead carried a record-player to the fantail of his ship, and a moment later the sound of music came floating down the column from across a mile of open water, sounding true and clear and close. It was a soft, nostalgic song, "You'd Be So Nice To Come Home To."

On every ship in line, men stood motionless in the spell of it all, listening quietly, each caught up in his own thoughts.

The song ended. But the spell did not, for the next ship in line took up where the destroyer had left off, and down the line there came the music of another record, so that all of the men on all of the ships were listening to still another song of the melancholy loneliness of war, "When the Lights Go On Again, All Over the World." It passed on then to the next ship, and to the heartbreak of "Lili Marlene." Then it came to us for our turn, and we played "As Time Goes By." So it went, all the way down the column—"I'll Be Seeing You"—"My Sister and I"—"Bluebirds over the White Cliffs of Dover"—"The Last Time I Saw Paris"—all the sad soft songs of the war, of sorrow made bearable by hope. It was all impromptu, all done without plan, but it was a thing of beauty and near-perfection, as each crew in turn passed along one clear song to serenade the other crews across the water.

Finally, it reached the British destroyer on the far end of the column, and drifting up through the dusk came the tender notes of "My Shining Hour." Then it all stopped, just as all good things should stop when they are at their best. The twilight gave way to night shadows, and we sailed along in silence, with a deep longing for peace and for home.

From there on, there seemed to be a poignancy to that crossing that had not been with us on our earlier voyages. All of us felt, I suppose, that we would not have much more time together, that with war strength rising to its crest in Britain, and with the Channel invasion coming at any hour, the convoys as we had known them would soon be dissolved.

There would still be ships carrying men and supplies, of course, for a long time to come, long after the invasion itself. They would be going into ports that we had never entered, into places like Cherbourg and Antwerp, and probably in time into Bremerhaven and Hamburg. But that would not be the convoy war that we had known.

We had won our personal war, the Battle of the Atlantic. We knew that there could never be a replay of what the convoys had done in that struggle, not in this war nor in any other that might come along in the future. We were about to end our part, to disperse and go our separate ways, with the memory of something that had become our special own.

All the way back across the ocean on that voyage in midspring, 1944, we reminisced over our coffee and on watch, talking of other crossings and other convoys and of lone voyages without convoys. The incidents that we recalled, the amusing ones and the sad ones and the grim ones, seemed endless—

We remembered that day in the Mediterranean when a British submarine found herself crippled and unable to dive, and tried desperately to join us for protection. But every time she drew near with her frantic signals, we mistook her for an enemy and greeted her with gunfire, until finally a British frigate got to the scene, saw what was going on, drew alongside, and explained the whole awkward situation. After that, the submarine moved up and hung so close to our stern that we had trouble throwing garbage overside without hitting her.

Then there was the memory of the Polish destroyer that had crossed the Atlantic with us twice in the worst days of submarine warfare. She was a trim ship, we recalled, skippered by a Polish naval officer who had lost his family and his estates to the savagery of the German Army. For revenge, he had delivered his ship to the Royal Navy and applied for convoy duty. The legend was that he and his Polish crew never took a prisoner from a sinking submarine—that they eagerly took German survivors aboard, but only for the specific purpose of throwing them back in again, while saving a few to be hanged from the rigging. He had his ship painted salmon pink, so that the German submarine commanders would recognize it and know what to expect.

I could never confirm the stories of murder, but I know he was there with his pink ship. We spent several weeks with him.

There was the memory of going ashore one time with a skipper and a chief engineer from another ship, and visiting a Belfast pub. We left the skipper there when we wanted to move along to other pubs, because he insisted on staying to settle an argument that was raging among Irishmen at the next table. After we had gone, he discovered that the Irishmen did not want their argument settled. They got that point across by picking him up and throwing him bodily through the pub's plate glass window.

There was the time at Heysham, I recalled, when my gunners went off on shore liberty and found a public dance going on at a local hall. While most of them waited outside for a few minutes to comb their hair and check their fingernails for dirt, one gunner walked in by himself. His shipmates followed just in time to see him attacked by a group of RAF troops who had decided he was alone and who were on the point of throwing him out. The battle that followed just about took the dance hall apart. I had a busy time with the medicine chest that night when the gunners got back to ship, but they brought home a collection of RAF caps as tokens of victory.

Then there were memories of what a thrilling sight it was, no matter how many times repeated, to see a big convoy under attack by day, with its colorful flag hoists whipping in the breeze and showing bright in the sunlight, and with a hundred ships swinging into spray-whipped turns, forty-five degrees at a time, foaming through the high waves and the erupting waters in a spectacle of unforgettable brilliance and precision. And there were memories of the night attacks when the red and green lights on the "Christmas tree" signal bars took the place of the flag hoists, and you could see them flashing and gleaming through the darkness as the great ships leaned into their turns, with their guns spitting flame in the night.

There was the time, somebody remembered, when we passed a giant dead shark floating belly-up in midocean, and sitting all around him like guests at a banquet table were twenty sea gulls, precisely spaced and not touching the food, for all the world like dinner guests with their napkins ready, waiting for the host to make a speech or offer a toast or say Grace. Everything was so perfectly in order that you almost expected to see place cards and salad bowls in front of each bird.

Then there were the friendly whales that frolicked alongside and spouted at us in the northern seas, and the long, slender, and deadly sea snakes that swam beside us for a while as we sailed past Yemen in the Red Sea.

There was the time in the Mediterranean when we were carrying orders to put in at Bari, on the east coast of Italy. The orders were cancelled while we were on our way in, so we turned back and rejoined the convoy. The next day German bombers struck and the port of Bari was blown to rubble.

There were memories of songfests in the London subways when we were trapped there by air raids; of getting home to New York one time after a long and dirty trip and then being ordered out to sea again after exactly twenty minutes in a hotel bedroom; of composing parodies on John Masefield's poetry after a particularly embarrassing attack when we did almost everything the wrong way—

> Awkward little convoy, signals all haywire,
> Churning the Atlantic, bumbling as you go—
> With a cargo of airplanes, gasoline and powder,
> TNT and dynamite, ready to blow.

So it went, on that westward crossing in midspring of 1944, a time of reminiscing, of looking back across the months, all the way back to Little Creek where it had all begun. For now there was the feeling that it was soon to end, and that nostalgia would one day soften the memory of the moments that had been terrible, and brighten the memory of the good moments, the friendships, and the strange fascination of the far seas and the distant harbors.

It was a quiet crossing. If there were any submarines abroad on the convoy lanes that month, they left us alone.

At sundown one warm evening, when we were just north of Cape Cod, the British destroyer that had been leading us in the Irish Sea serenade two weeks earlier broke from its escort position, turned, and came through the convoy columns until she was alongside our ship.

"We have orders for you to leave convoy and go into

Boston," she called across on the bullhorn. "It was nice knowing you. We're going home now."

She cut away at high speed to sweep back down the convoy column, and as she went off on her own, her record-player swung into loud action again. She foamed away toward the distant horizon, trailing behind her the rollicking tones of "The Campbells Are Coming."

To Boston, then. We swung out of column and let the other ships surge by, and then we put the wheel hard right and straightened out for the run to port.

On the way in, we received a radio message from Commander Eastern Sea Frontier: "Burn dimmed running lights after dark tonight."

No more coastal blackout? Things were really looking up.

CHAPTER TWENTY-TWO

RENDEZVOUS

THE TIME HAD COME. WE KNEW IT ON THAT HOT Wednesday morning, the seventeenth of May in 1944, when we moved out past Boston Light in a small convoy of twenty-eight ships. This, we knew, was the start of a voyage that would grow and expand and embrace thousands of other ships until it soared at last to a climax of invasion.

We had loaded at the Army base pier in South Boston. Our decks were jammed with tanks and trucks and artillery pieces. Our cargo holds were crammed to their last foot of space with bombs and shells and food and medicine. The gun crew magazines had been packed so close to the limit with ammunition that we would have had trouble making room for one more 3-inch shell. We had been issued special gas masks, and special rubber suits for protection against possible biological warfare attack.

We were on our way for a rendezvous with that long-sought D-Day hour somewhere on the coast of France, when all the months and years of convoy work would peak to their reward with the landing of weapons, men, and supplies on a beachhead battleground.

We sailed north to Halifax for our convoy conference, moving in toward the harbor on a Friday evening, and watching the smoke from Nova Scotia forest fires drift lazily down over the tall pine woods and the rocky coast-line. By early Sunday morning, we were on our way out again, slipping past the submarine nets, heading out to where the flat open sea awaited us and where the sun beat down with such brassy heat that we walked about the decks in nothing but our shorts.

On the following day at noon, we met the New York section of the convoy, and joined up and straightened out for the voyage across to Europe. If any man had doubted that we were moving toward an invasion, that was the moment when he quickly rearranged his thinking.

Never in all the months of our voyages had we ever seen such massive power afloat on the Atlantic. We were close to 200 ships in all, and that included fully thirty warships and three aircraft carriers. As we moved into final formation for the crossing, we stretched out into a vast, foaming front that was seventeen columns wide, spreading from north to south across ten miles of ocean.

We had tankers and freighters. We had tough-looking, snub-nosed ocean tugs. We had luxury liners that were jammed with troops. We even had shallow-draft, New England coast excursion steamers that were never built to withstand ocean waves but that would be ideal for ferrying combat men from English ports to the beachheads on the far side of the Channel. We were probably the strangest assortment of ships that ever crossed the sea in a single group, and yet we were a fleet that seemed almost to vibrate and sing with power. Wherever we looked, we saw ships so heavily packed with fighting equipment that at times it seemed the decks would be awash.

All day long, the planes from the three carriers roared

overhead like hornets, swinging far out to the convoy's flanks and far out over the course ahead, always on the hunt for submarines.

And the U-boats were there. They had not bothered us on the westward voyage to Boston, for at that time our convoy had meant nothing to them. But now, this convoy and any others like it meant a living, frightening threat to Germany's Atlantic wall, and if possible the ships must be stopped.

But that was not possible, not at least with anything the U-boats could throw at such a formidable number of guns and bombs and aircraft and warships and depth charges.

Still, they made the attempt. On our third day out, just as twilight was at its gloomiest and the sea was growing dark and vague, our escorts flashed the warning of submarine contacts from far out ahead of the convoy's port wing and just below the horizon.

The alarm lights went flickering across the broad columns, two green lights over a red, and the guide whistles blew their deep blasts, and we swung forty-five degrees to starboard and went surging off toward the night clouds that hung low in the southeast.

In a few moments we heard the roar of carrier planes, speeding overhead toward the danger point. After a time, looking through the glasses toward where a patch of dull red still lingered from the sunset, I could see two distant flashes, about five miles apart. Then the planes came back through the darkness and the Convoy Commodore flashed the All Clear signal, and we swung back to our normal course again.

For a while, then, we enjoyed a spell of smooth sailing,

with the sea calm and the sun warm by day and with the air soft at night. Soon we sailed into the cold grayness that comes with crossing the Labrador Current, and we rolled for a time in mildly rough seas that turned dark under the low, racing clouds. Then we were across the current and out on the far side, into the flow of the Gulf Stream with its sunshine and its warm breezes.

The U-boats stayed with us, lying back quietly until Saturday, when we had been at sea nearly one week. They began closing in, feeling for an opening, probing for a weak spot through which they might attack.

Three times that morning and twice in the afternoon, our escort ships broke out their submarine alarm signals, hoisting their big black pennants and circling off to drop an occasional depth charge to hold the submarines down. Finally, at twilight, they caught one of the undersea fleet just off the port wing of the convoy. Two destroyers and a corvette picked up the contact almost simultaneously and went racing to the spot on converging courses, with their long black pennants streaming out in the dusk.

They laid down a depth charge attack that fairly shook the bottom of the sea, and then came a crushing underwater explosion that jarred our ship to its hull plates. We stared at the spot of attack, waiting to see if a crippled submarine would break the surface. But all we saw was a heavy oil slick and chunks of debris that floated up from below and gradually spread far out across the waves.

That night, a bright moon glistened across a satiny sea, and out on a pattern of silver ripples our destroyers and corvettes fenced with a pack of U-boats that refused to be driven off.

Depth charges were dropped intermittently. The ocean would shudder and our ship would tremble as the concussion rose from below to the shining surface. We would sail on, silent except for the whisper of water cleaving at the bow and soft-spoken words on the bridge. Then another jar would shake the ship, and another, sometimes lightly as though from far away, sometimes heavily from close by. Through it all, the great convoy moved onward, silent and watchful and unstoppable, without changing course or altering speed. The gunners stood by their weapons, enjoying the warmth of the night and the shine of the stars and the clear reflections on the surface of the sea.

Next day, the submarines were still at hand. It was Sunday again, an idyllic day of warmth and peace and sunshine as far as nature was concerned. But a grim day in the ocean's depths. All through the morning and past noon, we sailed on a blue, rolling sea, with the destroyers and corvettes from time to time breaking the calm and the silence with their depth charge patterns. The submarines stayed low, so far down toward the ocean's bed that the carrier planes could not spot them, so far down that there was always a long delay between the time a depth charge went into the sea and the time when its explosive concussion would come rumbling up from the deep waters.

Once, in midafternoon, a destroyer caught one of the enemy too near the surface and directly ahead of the convoy and laid down a jarring, thundering pattern of ten depth charges. But the convoy ships held their positions, while the destroyer went curving off toward the horizon, flying the flag hoist that meant: "I am following an underwater contact. Stay clear."

After that, we were not bothered again until ten o'clock that night. Suddenly, the U-boats moved to close in under cover of darkness, and to angle themselves into a position that would leave the convoy ships silhouetted as black targets against the shine of moonlight. The escorts on the port wing spotted the maneuver and fired their white-flare alarm signals high into the night sky. We manned our guns, and the green and red lights flashed up and down the columns and we swung into a series of emergency turns. For a few minutes, the night's stillness was ruptured with the shriek of sirens, the blast of whistles, the sounds of shots and explosions and shouts. But an hour later, we swung back on course again and sped along on our way, smoothly and quietly, with every turn of our propellors carrying our huge cargoes of war supplies closer and closer to an unknown beach that had been marked for assault.

Finally, on the last day of May, as we neared the shores of Northern Ireland, the Commodore began to break up the convoy by sections, ordering some ships to Loch Ewe, some to the Clyde, others to Liverpool, and others to the Bristol Channel, all to wait in sheltered waters until the word came to move toward the Continent.

Our instructions were to proceed to Belfast Lough for orders. We moved into twin columns with other ships heading for the same port, and we began the familiar approach to the North Channel. It had been a good crossing, and now we relaxed on deck to enjoy the final leg of the voyage. As we lolled there, soaking up the sun's rays, the radio operator joined us with word on the latest news from London. Parts of the report dealt with our convoy; we learned that we had sunk two submarines on the crossing, and that our escort ships had picked up survivors from the second one.

At seven o'clock on Friday morning, we turned in from the sea, rounded the point of land below Whitehead, and moved toward our assigned position in the Belfast anchorage off Bangor. We gaped in awe because suddenly we were looking upon such a sight as no European port had ever seen before.

The harbor was an incredible picture of massed sea power. Close by our position were the battleships *Nevada* and *Arkansas,* the cruisers *St. Paul, Tuscaloosa,* and *Marblehead.* There were destroyers almost everywhere we looked—the *Plunkett, Murphy, Glennon, Welles, Butler, Gherardi, Herndon, Shubrick.* The British cruiser *Glasgow* lay off our beam, and beyond her was another cruiser and five British destroyers. There were French cruisers and Canadian destroyers and two aircraft carriers. There were familiar luxury liners, the *Britannic,* the *Colombie,* the *Santa Lucia* and half a dozen others. There were at least twenty tankers and sixty Liberty ships, the unglamorous but reliable veterans of the convoy lanes.

It was at once a staggering and beautiful sight, with the sun gleaming on the flags of a dozen nations, on the long-barreled guns, on the fine ships all swaying together at anchor, and all softly outlined against the green of the Irish hills and the blue ripples of the bay.

Within five minutes after our anchor went down, a launch from shore came alongside, and a work party led by a Royal Navy lieutenant scrambled aboard. They went about their jobs at once, stringing wires over the bridge, putting complicated new sets of signal lights into place, hammering and sawing, bolting unfamiliar name boards into position, boards with strange words like "Omaha" and "Easy Red" which meant nothing whatever to any of us. Then still another party came aboard, to check supplies with me and to make certain I was fully set with helmets and guns and ammunition stores and gas masks and rifles.

"Rifles?" I asked. "What in the world for?"

"You never know, old chap," they said. "Maybe the Admiral will stick you up in the bow to fire the first shot."

"When do we leave and where do we go?" I asked the Royal Navy lieutenant.

"That's an interesting question." He shrugged. "Old Jerry would like to know, wouldn't he?"

"What's a name like 'Omaha' doing in all this?"

He shrugged again. "I haven't the foggiest. I just come out here and stick up signs when and where they tell me to."

When at last he finished his work, and when all the new lights had been tested like Christmas tree decorations, he handed me a sealed envelope.

"All the best," he said. "I wish I could go along with you."

With that, he went back down the ladder into his launch and cruised away to start work on another ship.

The contents of the envelope told a simple story. We would depart sometime the following morning. The warships would go out first. We would receive a signal from shore when it was time to follow them. We would be given our port destination by radio on the following noon, a port on the south coast of England. There we would get our final orders.

That night, I stood for a long time on the wing of the

bridge, looking out across the massive fleet of ships and beyond to the soft, dark shapes of the Irish hills. I wondered in how many other harbors and bays and lochs there were other fleets like this one, and other men from Little Creek looking out at them and trying to grasp the tremendous reality that this was what it had all been for—all the nights of storm and attack, the deaths on the Murmansk run, the flaming tankers in the Caribbean, the men who drowned on their way to Malta, the ships that went down with their guns still firing, the ships that fought through to bring over the weapons and supplies.

Standing there, I remembered the words of an Admiral at a convoy conference in New York, many months before, when the war against the submarines was not going well.

"It is this simple," he had said. "If the Battle of the Atlantic is not won, the war against Germany cannot go on. The enemy can put 450 submarines against you. But you must outsink them. If you do, you will deliver to the armies the weapons and supplies they need. If you don't, there can never be an invasion of Europe, and we cannot possibly win final victory. That, in brief, is why you are here—and why you are going back out to sea, again and again and again."

Now it had been done. The submarines had been defeated, the supplies had been brought across, and our big task was over. Because of that, thousands of ships were lying quietly at anchor on this dark night, waiting for dawn and for the signal that would start moving the massive invasion machine toward its final rendezvous.

Seeing it all now, it was impossible not to feel a deep sense of pride, not to feel grateful for the privilege of having sailed the convoy lanes on such a mission, and yet more grateful for having survived.

With all that it had been, there would always be much to remember—the quiet darkness with ships all around, the sound of a sad harmonica coming from the gunners' quarters, the closeness to the stars above and the sea below as though the world had no other dimensions, the gratification of feeling another voyage done, the pain of seeing another ship go down, the emotions of fury and triumph and loneliness and fear. There would be thousands of memories to return unexpectedly in the years ahead.

Here it was now at its fulfillment, all symbolized in one dark harbor, all wrapped up for the story's end.

I listened for a little while longer to the sound of water lapping gently against the ship's hull and to the sigh of taut lines as the ship eased with the tide.

Finally I went below to my cabin to get some sleep, for it was after midnight—we were already into the early hours of June 3—and I had no way of knowing what tomorrow would bring, or the days that would follow in the coming week. Perhaps I would need all the sleep I could get. I turned in, lying awake in the darkness for just a minute or two and watching the stars through the open porthole overhead.

A few hours later, when darkness was just starting to fade toward light, I awoke to a tapping on my door. It was the petty officer of the watch.

"They've just started to move, Lieutenant," he said. "The ships are going out. Daylight pretty soon."

I dressed and went out on deck, and stood for a while watching the great, gray shapes of the warships as they glided by in single line, and rounded the distant point to move south toward the Channel ports of England, just across from Normandy's waiting coast.

I looked at the ships that were still lying quietly at anchor, the sea-worn tankers and Liberty ships of the convoy lanes. They were not moving yet. But they would be ready to go when the call came. They always were.

INDEX

Segment**238** INDEX

About the Author:

WILLIAM G. SCHOFIELD was a naval officer during World War II and is now a Captain in the Naval Reserve. He has been chief editorial writer for the *Boston Traveler* since 1952 and between foreign assignments has found time to do radio and TV broadcasts and to write nine successful books and a number of magazine articles. Mr. Schofield is married, has three children, and lives in Newtonville, Massachusetts.

PRINTED IN U.S.A.